Forensic Accounting and Financial Statement Fraud, Volume II

Forensic Accounting and Financial Statement Fraud, Volume II

Forensic Accounting Performance

Zabihollah Rezaee

BEP BUSINESS EXPERT PRESS

Forensic Accounting and Financial Statement Fraud, Volume II: Forensic Accounting Performance
Copyright © Business Expert Press, LLC, 2019.

First published in 2019 by
Business Expert Press, LLC
222 East 46th Street, New York, NY 10017
www.businessexpertpress.com

ISBN-13: 978-1-94999-107-9 (paperback)
ISBN-13: 978-1-94999-108-6 (e-book)

Business Expert Press Financial Accounting, Auditing and Taxation Collection

Collection ISSN: 2151-2795 (print)
Collection ISSN: 2151-2817 (electronic)

Cover and interior design by S4Carlisle Publishing Services Private Ltd., Chennai, India

First edition: 2019

10 9 8 7 6 5 4 3 2 1

Printed in the United States of America.

Abstract

Forensic accounting is gaining considerable attention as a rewarding and exciting field of accounting. Forensic accountants perform both fraud and nonfraud services. The organization of the book provides maximum coverage and flexibility in choosing the amount and order of materials on forensic accounting and financial statement fraud (FSF) theory, education, and practice. This book is organized into two volumes; each volume can be utilized separately or in an integrated form. The first volume, entitled "Fundamentals of Forensic Accounting" consists of five chapters presenting a road map for various fraud and nonfraud services performed by forensic accountants. The second volume, entitled "Forensic Accounting Performance," consists of five chapters addressing fraud and nonfraud forensic accounting practices and performance. Chapter 1 discusses roles and processes of forensic accounting. Chapter 2 describes forensic accounting techniques. Chapter 3 describes roles and responsibilities of corporate gatekeepers including forensic accountants in creating a corporate culture of integrity and competency in preventing and discovering financial statement fraud. Chapter 4 presents challenges and opportunities in forensic accounting in the areas of litigation consulting and expert witnessing. Chapter 5 discusses emerging issues in forensic accounting.

Keywords

forensic accounting; financial statement fraud; fraud examination; expert witnessing; litigation consulting; skill sets of forensic accountants; professional standards; codes of professional conduct; fraud and non-fraud forensic accounting services; corporate governance; antifraud policies and practices; challenges of forensic accounting; digital forensics; emerging issues in forensic accounting

Contents

Preface

Financial statement fraud (hereafter, FSF) is a severe threat to investor confidence in financial information and thus capital markets. Reported financial scandals by high-profile companies (Enron, Global Crossing, Qwest, WorldCom, Parmalat) and ethical debacles in corporations have eroded investor confidence and public trust in corporate America, its corporate governance, financial reporting, and audit functions. These scandals and related FSF reinvigorated interest in education and practice of forensic accounting and financial statement fraud examination. Forensic accounting is gaining considerable attention because the American Accounting Association (AAA) has added a new educational and research section on "Forensic Accounting," the Securities and Exchange Commission (SEC) has strengthened its FSF divisions and trained its staff in the area of forensic accounting and financial statement fraud, all international public accounting firms have established a forensic accounting department, and forensic accounting and fraud examination is becoming one of the fundamental components of business school's curriculum in recent years.

This book presents a comprehensive framework of the theory and practice of forensic accounting investigation and FSF examination in two volumes. The purpose of this book is to present a comprehensive primer of forensic accounting in areas of fraud and nonfraud services. At present, headlines have again been dominated by the investment Ponzi schemes and credit crunch scandals. Banks have been hit by record levels of fraud over the past several years, and the situation is likely to get worse as the full impact of the credit crunch unfolds. In such increasingly unstable economic and litigious environment, there has been significant growth in the demand for and interest in forensic accounting services. During the 2007–2009 global financial crisis, the focus on financial statement fraud prevention and detection become more important as regulators, investors, and companies seek better understanding of corporate malfeasance and misconduct.

In this book, forensic accounting is defined as the practice of rigorous data collection and analysis in the areas of litigation support consulting, expert witnessing, and fraud examination. Furthermore, forensic and investigative accounting services range from expert report preparation to appearing in the witness box, and from carrying out a fraud investigation to interviewing witness and securing evidence. As a rapidly growing area within the accounting profession, forensic and investigative accounting has gradually been recognized by professionals and academics. Forensic accounting is viewed as one of the most secured career tracks. There appears to be a gap between forensic and investigative accounting practice and education given that there is only a limited number of forensic accounting modules/courses offered within accounting and business curricula in universities worldwide. This book is intended to develop an awareness and understanding of the main themes, perspectives, frameworks, and issues pertaining to forensic and investigative accounting. This book provides practitioners, academics, and students with the knowledge and the professional and personal skills in technical, analytical, and communication areas to equip them to become successful forensic accountants with adequate knowledge in FSF examination.

The two volumes of this book present the essential and fundamental aspects, structure, theory, and practice of forensic and FSF, with a keen focus on a holistic approach in forensic accounting and fraud investigation. These two volumes should assist forensic accountants and fraud examiners with adequate knowledge and tools in effectively performing fraud and nonfraud forensic accounting services. Anyone who participates in the preparation of financial reports or uses financial information in making financial decisions should be interested in this book. Specifically, corporations and their executives, the boards of directors and audit committees, internal and external auditors, accountants, governing bodies, users of financial statements (investors, creditors, pensioners), business schools, other professionals (attorneys, financial analysts, bankers), forensic accountants, and fraud examiners will benefit from this book.

Sincerely,
Zabi Rezaee
January 15, 2019

Acknowledgments

I acknowledge the Securities and Exchange Commission, the Public Company Accounting Oversight Board, the American Institute of Certified Public Accountants, the Big Four Accounting Firms and Corporate Governance Organizations, American Accounting Association, American Certified Fraud Examiner, and other forensic accounting organizations for permission to quote and reference their professional standards and other publications.

The encouragement and support of my colleagues at the University of Memphis are also acknowledged. Especially, three of my graduate assistants, Mr. Charles Bell, Mr. Matthew Cantin, and Mr. Jon Paul Squitieri for providing invaluable assistance. I thank the members of the Business Expert Press team and S4Carlisle Publishing Services for their hard work and dedication in editing the book, including, Scott Isenberg, Mark Bettner, Michael Coyne, and Premkumar Narayanan.

My sincere thanks are due to my family, my wife Soheila, and my children Rose and Nick. Without their love, enthusiasm, and support, this book would not have come to fruition when it did.

Zabihollah (Zabi) Rezaee
January 15, 2019

CHAPTER 1

Roles and Processes of Forensic Accounting

Executive Summary

Forensic accountants are often hired to investigate allegations of wrongdoing such as financial statement fraud (FSF), employee fraud, misappropriation of assets, misrepresentation of financial information, kickbacks, bribery, conspiracy, inside trading, valuation disputes, and money laundering, among other forensic accounting services. It is important for forensic accountants to understand the role of evidence, methods of gathering sufficient and competent evidence, evaluate evidence, reach conclusions, communicate findings, make recommendations, and testify before courts. This chapter discusses the roles of forensic accountants and processes of forensic accounting, including the types of evidence (i.e., direct and circumstantial), evidence-gathering procedures, evidence assessment, conclusions, opinions, recommendations, and testimony.

Introduction

Forensic accountants gather evidence by conducting evidence-gathering procedures, evaluate evidence in terms of sufficiency and competency, use evidence in forming opinions, communicate their opinions, make recommendations, and testify in courts about their opinions. This chapter presents fundamentals of forensic accounting in performing fraud and nonfraud services by examining the types of evidence (e.g., direct, circumstantial, testimonial, physical, and documentary), rules of evidence, methods of gathering and evaluating evidence, and reaching evidence-based conclusions. The expertise of forensic accountants is in higher demand than expected in the areas of expert witnessing, litigation consulting, and fraud investigation, because the advancement of technology has augmented the specialized skills of forensic accountants. The increasing prevalence of fraud justifies the growing demand for and interest in forensic accounting.

The Role of Forensic Accountants

Forensic accountants, also known as investigative auditors or forensic auditors, are professionals that are usually employed to investigate financial and nonfinancial matters owing to a dispute, fraudulent, or imminent legal proceedings. Effective performance of forensic accounting services require gathering of a huge amount of both structured (e.g., general ledger or transaction data) and unstructured data (e.g., e-mail, voice, or free-text fields in a database), together with an increasing amount of nontraditional data sources such as third-party watch lists, news media, free-text payment descriptions, e-mail communications, and social media. Data analytics with the use of Big Data has been employed by forensic accountants to transform unstructured data into useful, structured, and relevant information for decision making in performing forensic accounting services. Forensic accounting services are often performed by individuals, with multidisciplinary knowledge and experience in accounting, technology, criminology, psychology, and laws, who are professionally skeptical in asking the right questions, utilizing data science and data management expertise to translate questions into meaningful analytics and use systems and information technology (IT) infrastructures.[1]

Individuals performing forensic accounting services are often working with professionals that are considered to have certifications such as the Certified Public Accountants (CPA), Certified Forensic Accounting Credential (CFAC), Certified Fraud Examiner (CFE), Forensic Certified Public Accountant (FCPA), Certified in Financial Forensics (CFF), and Certified Valuation Analyst (CVA), among others. These certifications enhance forensic accountants' competency, skill sets, and reputation. The new AICPA proposed standards, released in December 2018, classify forensic accounting engagements as services provided by members for "investigation" or "litigation".[2] The investigation engagements are services performed to reach a conclusion regarding concerns of wrongdoing in which the CPA performs necessary procedures to collect, analyze, evaluate, or interpret evidence on the merits of the concerns. The litigation engagements are actual or potential litigation services performed in connection with the resolution of disputes between parties in which the engagement does not need to be formal and may include alternative dispute resolution forum.

Forensic accountants should obtain sufficient understanding of how to plan and prepare for a forensic engagement, including considerations of whether to accept an engagement, defining the terms of the engagement, working with attorneys, identifying and managing resources, planning the engagement, and conducting the investigation. Accepting an engagement is an important step in the process of performing forensic accounting services. Forensic accountants base their opinion on the evidence gathered during their investigation. For example, a fraud investigation is the process of examining allegations of fraud, gathering convincing evidence, and reaching a resolution on the basis of evidence, reporting, testifying, and detection and prevention. Evidence is used as the foundation of a fraud examination, which is the basis for reaching conclusions. The evidence needs to be thorough, sufficient, competent, and credible in nature for the investigation to be appropriate. The sufficiency of the evidence is a matter of quantity about how much evidence is enough. The competency of the evidence is a matter of quality regarding whether the evidence is persuasive and credible.

The two main types of sufficient and competent evidence are documents and witness statements. The evidence should be evaluated and used as a basis for forming an opinion and writing a report. The report details the investigative process and the findings from the evidence used. Information often included in fraud reports are activities of the perpetrator(s), findings, and suggestions for improvement. Forensic accounting reports should be submitted to the interested parties. After the report has been issued, forensic accountants may be required to testify in court regarding the report and its findings. When testifying, the forensic accountant must take an oath to be honest and clear in communication and opinion.[3] The effective planning for fraud and nonfraud forensic accounting services requires that forensic accountants understand the scope, type, and motives of fraud explained in the following sections.

Fraud Models

The nature, scope, and drivers of fraud can be defined in many ways, including the fraud triangle. The fraud triangle was initially conceptualized by Donald Cressey (1953) and consists of three components—incentive, opportunity, and rationalization.[4] Fraud occurs when there are pressures or incentives to engage in fraud, opportunities to commit the fraud, and there is a rationalization for the actions taken; these can either be real or simply perceived by the fraudster. The American Institute of Certified Public Accountants (AICPA) issued the *Statement of Auditing Standards No. 82 (SAS No. 82)*[5] and then SAS No. 99, "Consideration of Fraud in a Financial Statement Audit" in 2002,[6] which promotes the fraud triangle as a theoretical framework in the investigation of FSF. The fraud diamond was later developed by Wolfe and Hermanson (2004) who added "capability component" as the fourth dimension of the fraud diamond.[7] The fraud diamond model includes incentives/pressures, opportunities, rationalization, and capability. The fraud pentagon model consists of five components—pressures/incentives, opportunity, capability, rationalization, and accountability. The inclusion of enforcement/compliance was introduced by Hossain, Mitera, and Rezaee (2016).[8] Exhibit 1.1 (Panels A, B, and C) presents all three models—fraud triangle, diamond, and pentagon—and they are further explained in the following paragraphs.

Exhibit 1.1

Models of Fraud

Panel A: Fraud Triangle

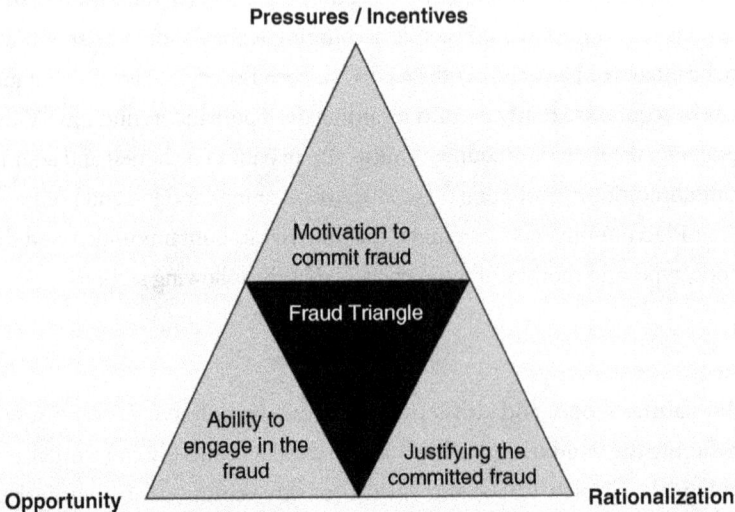

Panel B: Fraud Diamond

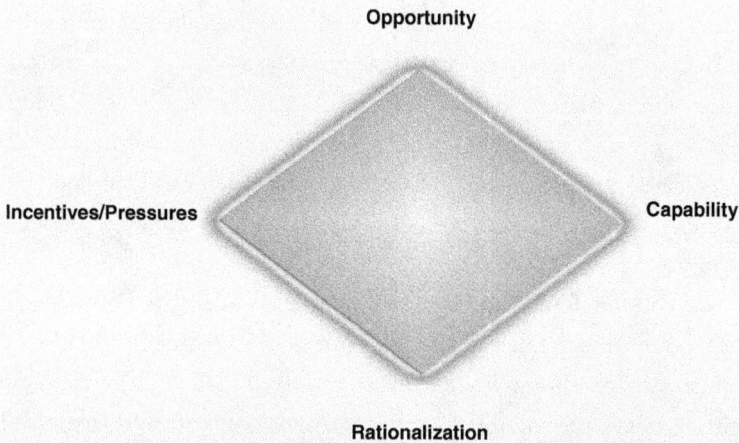

Opportunity

Incentives/Pressures   Capability

Rationalization

Panel C: Pentagon Model of Financial Reporting Fraud

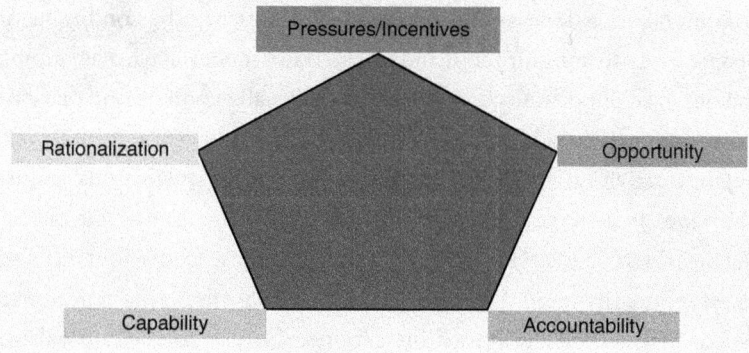

Pressures/Incentives

Rationalization   Opportunity

Capability   Accountability

Incentive is the motivation driven from conflicts of interest or a perceived pressure on individuals to commit FSF. In a corporate setting, incentive is typically examined in the context of operational/financial characteristics and as a motivating factor for management to adopt aggressive accounting policies and practices. Opportunity describes the conditions or corporate culture and environment that would allow management to commit FSF, which is often examined in the context of corporate governance effectiveness, adequate regulatory reforms, and vigorous enforcement of laws, rules, and regulations. Rationalization is a process by which management justifies its action in committing FSF and it can be addressed through psychological effects or mistakes in judgments in assessing the consequences of compromising ethical values or committing wrongdoings. Whereas incentive has been examined through the existence of internal and external pressures on management to achieve earnings targets or beat analyst earnings forecast and opportunity has been investigated through board and audit committee effectiveness and audit quality, rationalization has been difficult to examine because it is not easily measured.

To commit fraud, the fraudster must have adequate knowledge of the accounting systems and how they interact. Alongside the fraud models are four conditions that increase the likelihood of a person committing fraud; they are pressing financial need, opportunity, reasonable justification, and a lack of moral principle. The most serious of these aforementioned conditions is the lack of moral principle. This fraudster sees nothing wrong with committing fraud and will often continue to commit fraud as long as the opportunity is present. The conditions of people likely to commit fraud and all the fraud models have overlapping themes. The opportunity to commit fraud usually comes from a lack of or ineffective internal controls. Ineffective controls include the ability to override activities, no password constraints, and no preventions against collusion. If there is a strong separation of duties and multiple checks for areas with higher inherent risk, it is harder to commit fraud and easier to identify fraud. Rationalization, or justification, can stem from a real or perceived slight against the employee. It can also be rationalized by the employee by perceiving that the act is not actually stealing from the company. Also, the employee thinking that he or she is not hurting anyone or will be able to pay back the money before it is been noticed is also popular rationalization. This is important for forensic accountants to consider, so they can adequately examine the situations they are involved.

The pentagon model of financial reporting fraud (FRF) consists of five components: pressures/incentives, opportunity, capability, rationalization, and accountability through enforcement and compliance with all applicable laws, rules, and regulations. FRF occurs for a wide variety of reasons, more so when motives combine with opportunities.

Corporate strategy to meet or beat analysts' earnings forecasts pressures management to achieve earnings targets. Managers are motivated, in most cases, by pressure and reward when their bonuses are tied to reported earnings. This may induce managers to adopt accounting techniques that may often result in misreported earnings. Companies are more likely to engage in FRF when their actual earnings are predicted to fall short of certain thresholds. In such a situation, managers have incentives and pressures to manipulate earnings and engage in FRF by exercising their accounting discretion/flexibility available within the bounds of accounting standards. This is more likely when the benefits of manipulating earnings outweigh the associated costs and risks imposed by the adverse consequence of such frauds being detected.

The accountability element of the pentagon model of FRF is an extension of the fraud triangle model. All three factors—opportunity, incentive, and rationalization—*must* be in place for fraud to occur, and fraudsters must be able to commit fraud. Although the above-mentioned fraud elements deal with FRF prevention and detection, the accountability component is more relevant for FRF deterrence. The deterrence of FRF can be achieved when fraudsters realize that they will pay for the crime either through capital punishment or alternative severe criminal and civil penalties. The fifth component of FRF deterrence—"prevention and detection"—is accountability measured by effective compliance and vigorous enforcement of antifraud policies and procedures as well as severe punishment of fraud predators. Rezaee and Kedia (2012) present the following antifraud policies, procedures, and best practices of corporate gatekeepers, including the board of directors, management, internal auditors, and external auditors.[9]

The board of directors should establish the "tone at the top" by promoting competent and ethical behavior throughout the organization, effectively evaluating management performance and compensation as related to risk assessment, and vigilantly overseeing the financial reporting process and internal control system in preventing and detecting FRF. Management must design and implement an effective financial reporting process and internal control system while establishing a proactive approach to deter, prevent, and detect FRF. Internal auditors should provide both assurance and consulting services to their organization in the areas of operational efficiency, risk management, internal controls, financial reporting, antifraud, and governance processes. External auditors should provide reasonable assurance that financial reports are free from material fraud by integrating forensic procedures and fraud risk into audit strategies and tests and establishing open and frank dialogue with the board, audit committee, and management about the organization's vulnerability to fraud.

FRF occurs for a wide variety of reasons, including when motives combine with opportunity. Corporations' strategies to meet or exceed analysts' earnings forecasts pressure management to achieve earnings targets. Managers are motivated and rewarded by achieving or exceeding target earnings, which can lead managers to choose accounting principles that may result in the misrepresentation of earnings. Companies are more likely to engage in FRF when quality and quantity of earnings are deteriorating, management has incentives and pressures to manipulate earnings, opportunities to engage in FRF exist, and management can have rationalized that the benefits outweigh the associated costs calculated using the probability and consequences of detection.

Economic incentives are common in FRF, even though other types of incentives such as psychotic, egocentric, or ideological motives may play a role. Pressure on management to meet analysts' earnings forecast may give them the perception that their only option is to manipulate earnings. Management evaluates the opportunity for earnings manipulation and the benefit of earnings management in terms of the positive effect it will have on the company's stock price against the possible cost of consequences of engaging in FRF and the probability of detection, prosecution, and sanction.

Antifraud roles and responsibilities of corporate gatekeepers are important because FRF is typically committed at the level of the top management team rather than lower management or employees. Senior executives are primarily responsible for fair presentation of financial statements, whereas the board of directors oversees the financial reporting process and auditors (external and internal) provide assurance regarding the reliability of financial reports. Both the 1999[10] and 2010[11] reports of Committee of Sponsoring Organizations of the Treadway Commission (COSO) find senior executives' involvement in the high majority of

FRF cases (i.e., 83 and 89 percent, respectively). When management has incentives to meet financial targets through earnings management and the opportunities to override internal controls exist, senior executives may engage in FRF as further explained in the next section.

Misstatements

Any material misstatements can result in fraud. Management fraud is a deliberate action by the management to mislead users of financial statements through preparation of materially misstated financial reports. These deliberate misstatements or omissions of amounts or disclosures of financial statements attempt to deceive users of financial statements, including shareholders, creditors, governments, and other stakeholders. There are two types of misstatements that can mislead investors and other users of financial statements. These two misstatements are "fraudulent financial reporting" and "misappropriation of assets" accompanied by misleading financial information. There are many types of fraud schemes including occupational fraud, in which employees defraud their employer, FSF, in which management defraud users of financial statements, and other frauds, including vendor fraud, supplier fraud, customer fraud, and digital fraud.

Fraudulent Misstatements

There are many ways in which misstatements can occur, and fraudulent financial statements can be committed, including (1) fictitious revenues, (2) timing differences, (3) concealed liabilities and expenses, (4) improper disclosure, (5) improper asset valuation, and (6) earnings management.

Fictitious Revenues

This scheme is used to overstate revenues during periods of financial distress and duress or to improve outlook for a given period. There are several ways of recording fictitious revenues, including false journal entries, inaccurate sales to existing customers, sales to fake customers, and round tripping. False journal entries typically take the form of a debit to accounts receivable and a credit to sales. This method is often supported by internally generated phony supporting documents to mislead auditors. Also, if other journal entries are not created to offset the imbalance created, auditors will easily identify the misbalanced accounting equation. Fictitious revenues can also be recorded by inaccurately accounting for sales to existing customers or by claiming sales to fake customers. Both schemes involve the forgery of documentation to support the fraudulent distortion of the financial statements. Forgery would be committed on documents such as sales invoices, shipping documents, and purchase orders.[12] Similar to other revenue schemes, patterns exist, such as revenue at the end of a period, customers outside of the industry, and increasing sales with a drastic decrease in cost of goods sold. The same fraud detection techniques used under revenue recognition fraud can be used for this scheme too. Round tripping occurs when a transaction proves to be of little benefit but is recorded as if it were beneficial.[13] According to the 2018 Report to the Nations by Association of Certified Fraud Examiners (ACFE), FSF schema had the greatest median loss at $975,000 per incident.[14]

Timing Differences in Revenue and Expense Recognition

The timing differences in revenue and expense recognition include the following schemes:

- Not matching revenues with expenses: The effect of this error overstates the net income of the company in the period in which the sales were recorded and understates net income when the expenses are reported.
- Early revenue recognition: The result of this not only leads to statement misrepresentation but also can serve as a catalyst to further fraud.
- Recording expenses in wrong period: The motivation of doing this comes from the pressures to meet budget projections and goods and lack of proper accounting controls.

Timing difference fraud, also known as cut-off fraud, includes the recognition of revenues before they were earned, postponing the recording of expenses and liabilities, and shipping merchandise to customers before the sale is approved or finalized. Under generally accepted accounting principle (GAAP), revenue is recognized when they are realized or realizable, when goods change ownership, or when services are rendered. The company could also keep the books open after the accounting period ends to accumulate more sales. The purpose behind these forms of fraud is, much like the previous form, to improve the apparent financial position of the company to encourage stock purchases, increase the availability of debt funding and decrease its cost, and to meet analyst forecasts of sales and net income. If the company of interest is avidly seeking funding through equity or debt, this could be a sign to carefully examine it for the aforementioned forms of fraud. Forensic accountants can uncover most forms of timing difference fraud by sampling a selection of transactions from the sales journal and inspecting the credit terms, comparing shipping documents and invoices for discrepancies, comparing invoice prices with published or established sales prices, or by simply verifying major sales. Forensic accountants can also look for increased shipping costs or decreased expenses near the end of the accounting period, indicating an irregularity that requires further assessment.[15]

Concealed Liabilities

Concealed liabilities, as the name suggests, involve hiding certain obligations from investors and the public to improve the apparent health of the company's balance sheet similar to special purpose entities that were created by Enron to hide liabilities. Liabilities can be concealed by either hiding their existence or creating fictitious journal entries indicating that they have been paid down or paid off completely. A key component of financial health of a business is the leveraging of debt to generate returns. However, there is a delicate balance of debt-to-equity in every industry and it is not uncommon for businesses to be overburdened by debt. If this is the case, management may hide certain debt obligations that harm buy-ins to the company or reduce access to additional debt borrowing.

Companies that are in poor financial health, because of exorbitant amounts of debt, are likely suffocated by fixed costs associated with debt financing. If a company, struggling to pay bills as they become due, does secure additional debt funding by concealing liabilities, it only makes the fixed cost burden greater, thus making their financial position even more precarious than before. Liabilities could also be shifted from short term to long term to improve working capital figures, consequently increasing the apparent liquidity of the company. Liquidity, or solvency, is a key metric evaluated by creditors when making the decision to lend company money. Misclassification of the term of liabilities can be identified by identifying debt that was reclassified near the company's fiscal year-end or in interim financial statements submitted to creditors with the purpose of obtaining additional debt funding.[16]

Improper Disclosure

The disclosure of financial and nonfinancial is crucial and often required by law such as SOX Act of 2002, SEC regulations and accounting standards. Disclosed information may include footnotes, nonfinancial key performance indicators (KPIs), and other important items located in public reports that could have an adverse effect on the company's financial position. Disclosure schema include failure to disclose related party transactions, asset impairments, liabilities, and material departures from GAAP.[17] Fraudulent behavior may frequently arise when the disclosures are manipulated to exclude pertinent information, mentioned earlier. This is often done by management to hide data that may dissuade investors from investing. If a subsequent event occurs after the balance sheet date but before the statements are filed, public companies are required to disclose the information if it is material.

The Sarbanes–Oxley (SOX) Act addresses many issues with disclosures to increase investor confidence in the accuracy and completeness of financial information of reporting by public companies. It has been noted by many experts that potential fraud schema can arise from the strict requirements of the SOX Act. Although less common, it is also possible that disclosures include fictitious or overstated benefits. For example, disclosing a harmful significant transaction in a positive manner to deceive investors, when the effect on the company's financial health will be negative, is considered as fraud.

Improper Asset Valuation

Valuation is the act of determining the intrinsic value of an asset. Improper asset valuation often involves the overstatement of an asset's value, positively skewing earnings. The primary areas where improper asset valuation occurs are inventory, accounts receivable, and business combinations. Inventory can be overstated by falsifying physical count, and inflating its cost, among others. Accounts receivable is typically manipulated by either recording fictitious and related transactions in the accounts receivable, failure to write off uncollectible accounts, or manipulation of allowances for doubtful accounts. When a company acquires another business, it typically revalues its assets. The company could choose to falsely write up the assets to increase total asset value.[18]

There are several reasons for overvaluation fraud to occur. First, financial ratios are often used by investors to evaluate company performance. If the ratio is below the industry average or poor in comparison to previous years, investors are less likely to buy into the company. Also, certain debt covenants might be contingent on the company maintaining certain financial ratios. If the company falls below a contractually agreed-upon threshold, the creditor has the right to recall the debt and demand repayment in full. Management may intentionally overinflate assets to make ratios such as return on assets (ROA) appear better. Second, when more investors buy into a company, upper management may receive a bonus or the value of stock they own could increase. This is another incentive to erroneously report an asset's or group of assets' value(s).

Earnings Management

Earnings management is defined as a process of managing earnings to achieve the desired or targeted earnings. It can be done legitimately in creating sustainable performance, or in manipulating earnings. Earnings manipulation can be achieved by using accounting techniques to produce financial reports that present an overly positive view of a company's business activities and financial position. Although accounting rules and standards often require management to make judgment calls, earnings management takes advantage of the gray areas of these standards and rules to inflate revenue and assets and manipulate liabilities and expenses.

Earnings management needs to be properly monitored after being implemented in a business. There are currently many methods a business can use to evaluate earnings. The methods usually fall under the purview of U.S. GAAP and therefore comply with accounting standards. These methods include inventory flow (e.g., first-in-first-out (FIFO), last-in-first-out (LIFO), and cost method), timing principles, estimates, and classification of earnings. These methods can conflict under certain circumstances and be used by management to manipulate earnings. For instance, when a company has financial statement items that are non-GAAP, they are excluded from earnings management. The reason for this is that the reconciliation of non-GAAP to GAAP standards can cause earnings management to become inaccurate and, in turn, a poor methodology for running a successful business.[19]

In summary, material misstatements in financial reporting can be classified into several categories. The first and most common scheme is the intentional manipulation of financial reports by management as discussed earlier. The second most common is the timing differences in revenue and expense recognition. The third category is concealed liabilities. The forth category is improper disclosures. The fifth category is improper asset valuation. The Public Company Accounting Oversight Board (PCAOB) released Auditing Standard (AS)2401 in 2003 and made amendments to the standard in 2015, which outlines the importance of this audit function when detecting FSF. During the audit, the auditor looks for fraud during financial statement analysis by assessing the risk of material misstatement and using the audit risk (AR) to establish the level of acceptable materiality and detection risk. The lower the acceptable detection risk to the auditor, the more the procedures required to verify the validity of audit evidence.[20] On December 15, 2012, Au-C section 240 became effective. This standard, established by the AICPA, is similar in nature to AS 2041 released by the PCAOB. It requires the auditors to consider the possibility of management committing FSF. The standard also lays out auditor's responsibilities, requirements, and objectives.[21]

Asset Misappropriation

The most commonly used method for concealing liabilities/expenses is through liability/expense omissions because it is easy not to record liabilities and expenses, which makes it more difficult to discover the related fraud. Perpetrators of liability and expense omissions often plan to conceal their fraud until it can be compensated with future sources of income. For example, by increasing the sale price in the future when the omitted expenses can be recorded. These types of fraud can be prevented through effective internal controls and can be discovered through abnormal changes in accounts payable by recording unusual transactions in the postfinancial statement date.

Fraud can be committed by intentionally overstating inventory by falsely increasing inventory value and decreasing cost of goods sold. The fraud perpetrator can conduct the fraud of overstating inventory. An effective inventory internal control system using just-in-time and perpetual system can prevent fraudulent inventory overstatements. Four types of tools to discover fraud include inventory physical counting, review of accounts receivable, aging report, and analytical procedures. Inventory counting involves using inventory scanners, physical counts, and inventory logs to compare estimated count with actual inventory count. Massive discrepancies can indicate inventory fraud. Accounts receivable is an account used to measure sales that have been completed but of which payment has not been received yet. Reviewing accounts receivable can determine if sales were recorded when the transaction(s) were not completed. An aging report is a methodology applied to accounts receivable that determines "how long" or the useful life of account receivable. The older the receivable, the less likely it is to be collected and thus, more allowance for uncollectible/doubtful accounts should be considered. Analytical procedures allow for in-depth analysis of factors that can impact inventory, cost of goods sold and accounts receivable.

Asset misappropriation, usually pertaining to occupational fraud, involves the theft or misuse of the organizations' assets and can be conducted by any employee, including management and even nonemployees. However, employees are usually the perpetrator of asset misappropriations, whereas management typically engage in FRF, including asset misappropriations. The four current classifications of asset misappropriation are cash schemes, accounts receivables, inventory, and fixed assets schemes. These are discussed in the following paragraphs.

Cash schemes include skimming, larceny, and fraud cash payments. Skimming is defined as removing cash from company hands before it enters into the record books (accounting software). This fraudulent behavior often affects the revenues/sales account and checkbooks. Cash larceny is the theft of money from an employer without consent of the employer and the intension to give back. Lastly, fraudulent cash payments occur when an employee (usually in a management position) disburses cash to others unrelated to the business dealings. Examples of this type of scheme include payroll alterations, check forgery, and unrelated business expense reimbursement. This type of scheme is also the most prevalent form of asset misappropriation.

Accounts receivable is also subject to varying degrees of fraudulent behavior. The types of schemes prevalent to accounts receivable are lapping, made-up receivables, and posting unnecessary credits. First, lapping is recording a payment twice or recording another payment after the money was already received. Relating to fictitious sales mentioned in the previous paragraph, fictitious accounts receivables are only created to match phony and fake sales account. The reason for this is most businesses use the accrual accounting system, which records a debit to receivable and credits sale revenue when a revenue transaction has occurred not when a cash collected. Finally, the improper use of discounts, returns, and allowance for uncollectible accounts is often misused. An employee can manipulate an account as it was written off and then pocket the money for personal use.

Inventory fraud schemes happen in many types and sizes of retail and manufacturing companies, particularly in big warehouses of various businesses. The most common schemes are inventory theft, selling scrap, and use of inventory for one's personal use. The final category of asset misappropriation is fixed asset schema. This is the manipulation of a company's property, plant, and equipment, usually for personal use or gain. Theft of smaller equipment such as drills, hammers, and other lightweight objects is frequent.[22]

Employee Fraud and Theft

Employee fraud is committed by employees other than owners and executives. Employees are much more likely to commit fraud according to ACFE's 2016 Report to the Nations.[23] The median loss attributed to employee occupational fraud was $65,000, the median loss for managers was $173,000, and the median loss for owners/executives was $703,000. The reason for the high disparity in the dollar amounts is due to executives being able to bypass and control functions of the corporation, allowing them higher opportunities for fraudulent activity. The losses were also attributable more to males than to females. Out of the 2,410 cases analyzed by the ACFE, males contributed a median loss of $187,000, whereas females contributed only $100,000.[24] In the past 3 years, there was about 10 percent increase in median loss for females and a 6.5 percent decrease for males. When comparing positions held in the company, the gender breakdown between males and females matches the overall losses stated earlier. Owners and executives of both genders were more likely to steal more from the company. When fraud is broken down by schema, males engaged in FSF and corruption, whereas females engaged more in asset misappropriation. For both genders, as age increased, so did the frequency of fraud. Also, the higher the level of education, the more likely an employee is to commit fraud. Overall, 82.5 percent of perpetrators are never punished for their actions.[25]

A key component to analyze regarding employee fraud is the method of detection used. The three most common detection methods were tips, management reviews, and internal audits with the average of 36.55 percent, 13.6 percent, and 15.3 percent, respectively.[26] Across the regions of the United States, South Africa, Asia-Pacific, and Latin America and the Caribbean tips were the highest surveying in at 37 percent, 37.3 percent, 45.2 percent, and 36.9 percent, respectively. The average for all four regions is 39.1 percent. Management reviews in all four regions, polled in at 14.3 percent, 10.2 percent, 13.1 percent and, 17.1 percent, respectively, for an average of 13.68 percent. Lastly, internal audit detection across all four regions sampled at 14.1 percent, 16.2 percent, 15.8 percent, and 19.8 percent, correspondingly, for an average of 16.48 percent. These methods differed between size of firm, confession, management review, and surveillance. Larger firms preferred tips and internal audit, whereas smaller firms favored external and minor internal activities such as external audits.[27]

Employee fraud can be prevented and detected in many ways as follows:

1. Sound code of conduct: A proper and effective code of conduct for employees promotes a corporate culture of integrity and competency. The code of conduct should provide guidelines for ethical behavior and accountability.
   a. The ACFE states in their Code of Ethics that any illegal activity or activity that leads to a conflict of interest between parties is strictly prohibited. This standard adheres strictly to professionalism, which is a positive quality associated with one's business career. It is also important for a CFE to remain a confidant in all times throughout his or her career. Accounting ethics strongly supports the foundational pillar of accountability and confidentiality.[28]
2. Implementing an effective system of internal control and establishing a system of checks and balances in preventing employee fraud: An effective system of internal control should prevent, detect, and correct any errors, irregularities, and fraud.
3. Policies and procedures in observing employee's behavior: Employees tend to be more ethical when they know there is an accountability system that monitors their behavior and actions without invading their privacy.

Identifying and Gathering Evidence

Evidence identification, gathering, and evaluation during legal matters and independent investigations are crucial. This section discusses various services that can be performed by forensic accountants and the type of evidence they need to gather to effectively support their decisions to be able to defend in the court of law. Forensic accountants need to know where evidence (paper and electronic) can be found and how it should be evaluated and processed. For example, more credible and persuasive materials need to be gathered for fraud allegations regarding revenue manipulation because the majority of FSF cases involved improper revenue recognition even though revenue manipulation could be the most expensive form of earnings management. Revenue manipulation is the most common type of FSF, even though it can be very costly because of the higher likelihood of receiving comment letters from the Securities and Exchange Commission (SEC), short interest, restatements, increased audit fees and unfavorable audit reports, litigation, investigations, sanctions by regulators and standard setters, and negative market reactions.

Management is also responsible for cash flows generated from operating, financing, and investment activities because cash flows determine stock prices, firm valuation, and debt-service capacity, eventually influencing costs of capital. Manipulation of cash flows from operations is most common. For example, management can manipulate cash flow by classifying operating leases as capital expenditures that could shift the payments from the operating section of the cash flow statement to the investing section.

Rules and Types of Evidence

Evidence can be defined as things, matters, or issues—physical, verbal, or electronic—that can be relevant in an investigation to support assertions, propositions, or factual statements. The rule of evidence is whether a case is held before a judge or a jury or whether it is presented in court. There are two general categories of evidence. First, the direct evidence that provides the existence of a fact under investigation without any need for inferences or presentation of any other facts. Circumstantial evidence is the evidence that requires an inference on the basis of indirect evidence. Each of these two categories of evidence can be further classified into testimonial, demonstrative, and real evidence.

Testimonial evidence is an oral declaration of fact or a written statement by witness that is used in trial. This witness could be involved in the subject of litigation, to an extent, or could be an expert witness hired to provide credible testimony regarding a matter requiring specialized knowledge. These witnesses are typically subject to cross-examination by the opposing side. The aim of the cross-examination would be to discredit the individual's testimony or credibility within the circumstances of the case.[29]

Demonstrative evidence, by definition, includes all evidence that is not substantive or testimonial in nature. This form of evidence is often meant to demonstrate or represent testimonial evidence in a physical form and is only admissible when it precisely mirrors the witness's testimony. Examples of this type of evidence are pictures, charts, and objects that can be used in litigation to support the case. Demonstrative evidence can be immensely useful when testimonial evidence is complex in nature, because it can provide a visual representation of the facts that can be more easily understood by a jury.[30]

Real, or physical, evidence simply relates to any object used in trial and litigation. It is similar to demonstrative evidence in the sense of its physical nature; however, this form of evidence is not generated from testimony. Real evidence can include an alleged murder weapon, narcotics, fingerprints, clothing, or any material object used to prove or disprove an issue in a trial. An important concept relating to real evidence is its chain of custody. This describes the chronological possession of the evidence, aiming to reduce the chance of admitting tampered or contaminated evidence into the trial.[31]

Evidence-Gathering Procedures

Forensic accountants perform a variety of investigative, litigation, and expert witnessing services for their clients that range from a simple asset valuation to a more complex fraud and dispute investigation. Regardless of the type and complexity of the engagement, forensic accountants should do the following steps of planning and preparation, evidence gathering and evaluation, and conclusions and communication.

Planning and Preparation

Forensic accountants should plan the engagement by deciding to accept the engagement, evaluate the client, obtaining an understanding of the engagement case, assess their resources and ability to perform the service, and the commitment to do thorough investigation. The decision to accept the client is extremely important, particularly in the case of expert testimony and requires proper negotiation and understanding of the scope of forensic accounting services. Forensic accountants should obtain either verbal or written agreement from their client before performing the service. Terms of the agreement should be specified in the engagement letter. During the planning stage, forensic accountants should consider the factors that increase the likelihood of FSF. These factors should be addressed and considered in planning an investigation absolute power, greed, incompetence, capability, pressures/incentives, opportunity, collusion, and lack of proper business codes of conduct. Factors that may decrease the possibility of FSF are effective corporate governance; compliance with applicable laws, rules, regulations, and standards; effective internal controls; and tone at the top.

Gathering Evidence, Reporting, and Court Proceedings

After the engagement has been planned, the forensic accounting team must gather evidence. In the current forensic landscape, there are various procedures that can be used to gather sufficient, accurate, reliable, and timely evidence. These procedures include testing controls, which can be used to identify security loopholes, and analytical procedures to conduct trend or comparative analysis. This will enable accountants to detect paradigms or cycles on a business using advanced computer techniques and software, interviewing, and reconciliations. The aforementioned processes will allow enough evidence to be gathered to report to the client. The report includes the fraud scheme and information supporting the schema. This report is used in court proceedings as evidence to determine the guilt, or lack therefore, of the defendant.[32]

Evidence-Gathering Methods

Brainstorming Sessions

Mind-mapping, open-ended, computer-mediated, and strategic reasoning are the four types of brainstorming techniques, according to the Tennessee Society of CPAs (TSCPA).[33] These methods each involve the forensic team holding meetings to create means to interact with fraud.[34] Opened-ended brainstorming involves practitioners selecting an arbiter that allows the free flow of ideas. A notetaker is present and is not allowed to participate in the discussion. This technique has a shortcoming though; not all ideas may be heard because of time constraints and number of individuals speaking per session. In relation to fraud, this technique is frequently cited has discovering fraud risk factors at a higher rate.

Computer-mediated brainstorming is the use of a computerized environment to simulate face-to-face interaction via electronic transmissions. Examples of this technique include telecommunications, Skype, and Blue Jeans. Electronic data transmission allows quicker exchange of information when compared with other methods. It also allows for anonymous transfer of information, if necessary. Mind-mapping is real-time diagramming placing the discussion title in the center and major elements branch from the center. This approach is evidence of the use of visualization technologies, which are becoming more prevalent as data sizes increase (Big Data). Both computer-mediated and mind-mapping uses software such as XMind, iMindMap, and StormBoard to host these visualizations and communication networks. Lastly, strategic reasoning evaluates how managers commit fraud. This perspective enables auditors to think in the shoes of management when conducting an audit and looking for fraudulent behavior.[35]

Red Flag Identification

Red flags are defined the early symptoms that would indicate a higher risk of potential fraud or intentional misstatement of financial statements. Forensic accountants can assess fraud by focusing on using fraud risk factors, "red flags," to assess the overall risk of fraudulent financial reporting as suggested in SAS No. 99.[36] In this approach, the forensic accountant identifies the presence or absence of certain red flags and then assesses the risk of fraud. To facilitate the use of red flags, various decision aids have been developed, such as checklists, regression models, and expert systems. One major limitation of current red flag approaches is that they are developed to assess the overall fraud risk without considering the impact of fraud schemes that are used by management to perpetrate and conceal fraud.

A checklist consists of a list of potential red flags that the auditor can use to assess fraud risk. Various decision aids have been developed, including checklists, regression models, and expert systems to facilitate the use of red flags. A checklist consists of a list of potential red flags or sympathies that forensic accountants can use to assess fraud risk. Checklists are the most common decision aid for forensic accountants. One major drawback of the checklist is that it ignores the structure and interrelations between fraud risk factors.

Examples of red flags checklists of FSF are:

- Personal financial pressure
- Vices (e.g., drugs, alcohol, or gambling)
- Extravagant lifestyles
- Real or imagined grievances against company
- Related parties
- Increased stress
- Internal pressures

Red flag lists are often used to spot and warn about fraudulent activity by degree of severity. A red flag is defined as a circumstance that is outside the norm. There are several categories of red flags that can enable forensic accountants to identify and detect errors, irregularities, and fraud. These categories include:

- Employee red flags: Can be identified by changes in expenses, turnover, working overtime frequently, or lack of separation of duties. For example, if an employee buys a Porsche not affordable with the salary made in the position held, this is an employee red flag.
- Management red flags: Signs include noncompliance with accounting standards and policies, lack of internal control environment, too many bank accounts, decisions made by a select few managers, too many year-end transactions, or nonresponses and waiver of auditors suggested adjustments and closing entries.
- Change in behavior red flags: This category can apply signs including borrowing money from coworkers, excessive drinking or other negative habits, carrying unusually large amounts of cash, overworking, or gambling beyond reasonable means.

Statistics have been released that enable forensic accountants and auditors to search for specific red flags. An overwhelming 42.1 percent of occupational fraud violations are committed by employees and 61 percent of fraudulent actions were perpetrated by males. Despite these statistics to help narrow down red flags, 88 percent of individuals who commit fraud are never caught by the legal system.[37]

Regression Models

The most common regression models are linear and logistic. Different model selections can be used with these regression types, including backward, forward, and stepwise. Regressions are often used to perform statistical analysis on data sets, in which relationships among input and target variables must be discovered. There are many software providers that produce software that aids in regression modeling. An example of regression software is SAS Enterprise Miner.[38]

A logistic regression model can be used in fraud detection by analyzing a company's financial information in a model to identify irregularities and anomalies for further inspection. For example, the timing of a company's journal entries could be examined using a linear regression model, where the relationship between number of journal entries of a specific category and time are analyzed. If the number of journal entries in specific accounts with a high propensity for fraud increases drastically at year-end, forensic accountants would be alerted to closely inspect that specific account for potential fraud. A predictive model can be used in a similar fashion by using historical data to project certain financial ratios. If the projected ratios are drastically different from the ratios on financial statements, that would be an indication for the auditor to see if the over- or underperformance caused by fraud.

Expert System Aids

Expert system aids are commonly computer-based design consultation systems that verify completeness, consistency, and accuracy of transactions or events. These computer-based expert system aids are often used to mimic the decision-making process and reasoning capabilities of the human mind. Forensic accountants can use expert system aids to increase the efficiency and accuracy of their work. Expert systems mimic the auditors' and forensic accountants' professional judgment to arrive at similar conclusions as the human. These systems are fed large amounts of test data and professional knowledge and reduced to "if-then" rules to build a basis for decision making and analysis. As expert systems have progressed over time, they are capable of processing increasingly complex issues and providing thorough solutions, similar to that of a human expert. The benefit of expert systems from a fraud detection standpoint is that forensic accountants are able to analyze 100 percent of the data in the area of interest to detect anomalies, in a significantly shorter amount of time.[39]

Analytical Procedures

Analytical procedures are techniques used by forensic accountants and auditors in gathering and evaluating evidence by studying plausible relationships between financial data and their link to nonfinancial data. Analytical procedures can be an effective tool for forensic accountants in all phases of an investigative engagement, including the planning phase of deciding on the extent and types of tests, in substantive testing of gathering and evaluating evidence, and in the overall review of an investigation in justifying results and opinions. Like auditors, forensic accountants can perform analytical procedures during the planning stage of the investigation to enhance understanding of the client's business and to assist in planning the nature, timing, and extent of their testing. During the planning stage, analytical procedures are typically performed by comparing financial data with nonfinancial data and developing expectation for the investigation. Forensic accountants' expectations should be developed through a comprehensive understanding of the client and its industry and knowledge of the client's financial and internal control systems. Forensic accountants may use several sources of information to develop expectations, including financial information from prior periods, nonfinancial information (client standing in the industry with peers, management style, and integrity), anticipated results (budgets or forecasts), information on the industry in which the client operates, and the relationships of financial information with nonfinancial information.

Financial ratios are often used to detect FSF. Research from the past 30 years has shown that specific ratios are more useful at fraud detection than others. The ratios of total debt-to-total assets (TD/TA), total liabilities-to-total assets (TL/TA), total debt-to-equity (TD/E), current assets-to-current liabilities (CA/CL), and working capital-to-total assets (WC/TA) have proven to be most effective in establishing relationship among financial data. Managers have more incentives to commit FSF when liquidity is low, and that the above-mentioned ratios aid in determining liquidity of a business. Financial ratios are typically classified into profitability, solvency, and operating ratios that enable forensic accountants to detect financial anomalies and items that are out of norm.

Scanning is an eye-open approach looking for unusual items and is considered as analytical procedure that relies on the professional judgment, which has been developed through education and work experience, to identify suspect items during an audit or a forensic investigation. These can include overstated or understated accounts, new accounts, and balances that are high or too low in comparison with the industry average.[40] A combination of financial ratio analyses, scanning, and time-series analyses can enable forensic accountants to identify unusual items and anomalies. For example, if a company has historically grown 5 percent annually, managers could be under pressure to misstate financial statements if the internally expected growth is less than 5 percent. Additionally, analyst projections can exacerbate the pressure felt by management, as often when the consensus of analyst projections is not met, the company is punished by the market with a fall in stock price.[41] A comparison of financial data with nonfinancial KPIs such as budgets can assist forensic accountants to establish benchmark for assessing management expectations and incentives.

Financial reporting analysis techniques can help detect FSF. The first is vertical analysis for analyzing the relationships between the items on an income statement, balance sheet, or statement of cash flows by expressing components as percentages. This method is often referred to as "common size" financial statement analyses. In the vertical analysis of an income statement, net sales are assigned 100 percent; for a balance sheet, total assets are assigned 100 percent. All other items in the financial statements are expressed as a percentage of these numbers. It is the expression of the relationship or percentage of component part items to a specific base item. Vertical analysis emphasizes the relationship of statement items within each accounting period. These relationships can be used with historical average to determine statement anomalies.

The second type is horizontal analysis, also known as "trend analysis," to determine changes (increase/decrease) in a series of financial data over a period of time expressed as either an amount or a percentage commonly over several years. The third type is ratio analysis, which is the study of relationship among financial items. Traditionally, financial statement ratios are used in comparison to an entity's industry average or other norms in identifying red flags of FSF.

Benford's Law

Benford's law, founded by Simon Newcomb, uses the occurrence of digits to show a trend.[42] The law compares the actual frequency of the digits in a data set, using a digit-by-digit approach. This output is compared with the expected occurrence to find holes in data. The deviations in the frequency are then investigated. For example, a forensic accountant may use Benford's law to spot fraud in an assigned case. The forensic accountant uses the standard Benford curve to identify an area for further investigation.

A Benford curve resembles an exponentially decreasing function, as it increases toward the y-axis and decreases as it moves away. Benford's law states that the number 1 will be the leading digit in a set of numbers approximately 30 percent of the time and the following numbers have a proportionally less chance of appearing as a leading number, relating to their respective order. A comparison between actual results and expected results can be analyzed simply by comparing graphs of the two. If the actual results do not approximately line up with the Benford curve, further investigation is needed. If a forensic accountant examines a large data set and finds that the number 1 is the leading digit only 8 percent of the time, it could be an indication that the data set is not genuine and fraud could be present.[43]

Artificial Neural Networks

Artificial neural networks (ANNs) are computer scientists' attempts in mimicking the thought process of a human brain in technology, which has proven success in detecting and preventing credit card fraud. The revolutionary feature of ANNs is their ability to model linear and nonlinear relationships, learn these relationships directly from the data being used, and apply them to future situations. Consequently, ANNs can be used as a tool in fraud detection, such as creating expectations for account balances that can be compared with actual balances. Previously used fraud detection systems would determine fraudulent events on the basis of a predetermined and static pattern; however, ANNs can gauge a transaction's variance from the pattern to determine a more accurate determination if the transaction is fraudulent.[44]

Forensic Data Analytics

Data analytics is the process of identifying, mapping, cleaning, examining, analyzing, and converting a set of raw data into formatted and useful information for decision making. This process is often conducted using specialized systems and software. Business organizations have increasingly used data analytics processes, techniques, and technologies as a decision aid to make more-informed business decisions. In recent years, Big Data analytics are employed to study and investigate large amounts of data to discover patterns, correlations, and other insights in the database as descriptive, predictive, or prescriptive modeling and analyses. Forensic data analytics help organizations by preemptively preventing fraud, improving internal controls, improving the regulatory and compliance environment, and controlling the degree of fraud reactively. Forensic data analytics provide forensic accountants with the predictive tools to deter FSF and establish fraud-protection solutions rather than attempting to manage damage after it has occurred.[45] The concept of Big Data and data analytics has been around for many years to capture and transform huge data into a set of manageable and useful information for decision making. Forensic accountants can use Big Data and data analytics to:

1. Discover patterns among data.
2. Connect the dots in discovering fraud.

3. Store large amounts of data.
4. Analyze new sources of data.
5. Effectively and efficiently, discover fraud.

The application of Big Data and data analytics to forensic accounting is currently at an early stage of initiation and development and forensic accountants have taken a scattershot approach in addressing capabilities of Big Data in identifying patterns in financial and nonfinancial information in annual and quarterly financial reports, management discussion and analysis (MD&A), and management earnings forecast. Forensic analytics is powerful enough to be used singularly, or alongside the practices of investigations, audits, and process review, and with such a large amount of data flowing in, forensic data analysis can be used to transform raw data into intelligible information.[46] It is expected that Big Data will grow bigger, and thus, forensic accountants should proactively search for patterns, including irregularities in Big Data, and assess and manage their risk profile in detecting fraud.

Forensic accountants can use Big Data, which has the capability to store huge amounts of data, and data analytics, the algorithms through which data are transformed to information, as valuable evidence. The use of both Big Data and data analytics is changing the way forensic accountants gather and assess evidence in their investigation and in discovering fraud. This affects planning, evidence gathering, and reporting phases of a forensic investigation. During the planning phase, forensic accountants should make sure to adopt some of the new tools that enable them to take full advantage of Big Data and data analytics. Forensic accountants should change their way of making decisions to take advantage of analytics. Building a foundation of Big Data and data analytics into the investigation process is now possible because of the new tools available. Forensic accountants have a wider set of options to use computerized-assisted investigation tools and techniques to perform descriptive and predictive analytics on Big Data in detecting fraud and providing early signals of fraud. The scale and complexity of Big Data, however, requires advanced levels of analytical skills by forensic accountants for data mining, deriving algorithms, and predictive analytics.

In summary, analytical procedures with the use of ratio analysis is the most conventional approach used in detecting fraud, despite its subjectivity in selecting the ratios that are likely to indicate fraud.[47] Data mining is another technique that can discover the implicit, previously unknown and actionable knowledge and include techniques such as logistic regression, neural networks, decision trees, and text mining. Time-series and regression analyses can be used to identify critical risk factors, financial and nonfinancial, and develops a regression model combining these factors to predict fraud. Expert systems, by incorporating judgment of auditors during the fraud risk assessment process, perform better than checklists or regression models.

Conclusion

In performing forensic accounting services of fraud investigation, expert witnessing, and litigation consulting, forensic accountants investigate allegations of wrongdoing such as FSF, employee fraud, kickbacks, bribery, conspiracy, inside trading, valuation disputes, and money laundering, among other forensic accounting services. It is important for forensic accountants to understand the role of evidence, methods of gathering sufficient and competence evidence, evaluate evidence, reach conclusions, communicate findings, write a report, make recommendations, and testify before courts. This chapter discusses fundamentals of forensic accounting, including types of evidence (i.e., direct and circumstantial), evidence-gathering procedures, evidence assessment, risk assessment, internal control evaluation, reach conclusions, express opinions, make recommendations, and testimony by the court.

Action Items

1. Rules of evidence determine whether evidence is permissible into various types of judicial and administrative proceedings.
2. Evidence is all things, matters, and issues relevant to the matter under investigation.

3. Evidence can be direct or circumstantial, physical, documentary, and verbal.

4. Evidence-gathering procedures are all methods of gathering sufficient and competent evidence.

5. Evidence should be used in forming an opinion and reaching conclusions.

6. Recommendations should be made on the basis of evidence gathered and opinion expressed.

Endnotes

1. Ernst and Young (EY). 2016. *Global Forensic Data Analytics Survey 2016. Shifting into Higher Gear: Mitigating Risks and Demonstrating Returns.* http://www.ey.com/gl/en/services/assurance/fraud-investigation---dispute-services/ey-shifting-into-high-gear-mitigating-risks-and-demonstrating-returns, (accessed January 4, 2017).

2. American Institute of Certified Public Accountants (AICPA). 2018. Exposure Draft: Statement on Standards for Forensic Services No. 1 (SSFS 1). Available at https://www.aicpa.org/interestareas/forensicandvaluation/resources/standards/exposure-draft-statement-on-standards-for-forensic-services.html

3. ACFE. 2018. *Planning and Conducting a Fraud Examination.* http://www.acfe.com/uploadedFiles/Shared_Content/Products/Books_and_Manuals/2018%20US%20FEM%20Sample%20Chapter.pdf, (accessed December 10, 2017).

4. D. Cressey. 1953. *Other People's Money: A Study in the Social Psychology of Embezzlement* (Glencoe, IL: Free Press).

5. American Institute of Certified Public Accountants (AICPA). 1997. *Consideration of Fraud in a Financial Statement Audit. SAS No. 82* (New York, NY: AICPA).

6. AICPA. 2002. *Statement on Auditing Standards (SAS No. 99): Consideration of Fraud in a Financial Statement Audit (November)* (New York, NY: AICPA).

7. D.T. Wolfe, and D.R Hermanson. 2004. "The Fraud Diamond: Considering the Four Elements of Fraud", *The CPA Journal* 74, no. 12, pp. 38–42.

8. M. Hossain, S. Mitra, and Z. Rezaee. October, 2016. "Can Capital Punishment Deter Financial Reporting Fraud," *Advances in Financial Planning and Forecasting* (AFPF), pp. 15–25.

9. Z. Rezaee, and B. Kedia. 2012. "The Role of Corporate Governance Participants in Preventing and Detecting Financial Statement Fraud," *Journal of Forensic and Investigative Accounting* 4, no. 2, pp. 176–205.

10. Committee of Sponsoring Organizations of the Treadway Commission (COSO). 1999. *Fraudulent Financial Reporting: 1987–1997, an Analysis of U.S. Public Companies* (New York, NY: AICPA).

11. Committee of Sponsoring Organizations of the Treadway Commission (COSO). 2010. "Fraudulent Financial Reporting: 1998–2007: An Analysis of U.S. Public Companies." www.coso.org

12. Wells, J.T. 2001. "Follow Fraud to the Likely Perp," *Journal of Accountancy* 191, no. 3, pp. 91–94. https://www.journalofaccountancy.com/issues/2001/mar/followfraudtothelikelyperp.html, (accessed September 11, 2018).

13. J. Ahmad, D. Jansen, and J.J. Frank. May, 2003. "Common Financial Statement Fraud Schemes," *Yale University*.http://faculty.som.yale.edu/shyamsunder/FinancialFraud/Frank-Common%20Financial%20Fraud%20Schemes%207May%2003v1.doc

14. ACFE. 2018. *Report to the Nations*. https://www.acfe.com/rttn2016/costs.aspx

15. J.T. Wells. 2001. "Timing Is of the Essence," *Journal of Accountancy*. https://www.journalofaccountancy.com/issues/2001/may/timingisoftheessence.html, (accessed September 12, 2018).

16. ACFE.2018.*Common Financial Statement Frauds*.https://brisbaneacfe.org/library/third-party-fraud/common-financial-statement-frauds/

17. Deloitte. 2009. *Sample Listing of Fraud Schema*. https://www2.deloitte.com/content/dam/Deloitte/in/Documents/risk/Corporate%20Governance/Audit%20Committee/in-gc-fraud-schemes-questions-to-consider-noexp.pdf, (accessed September 13, 2018).

18. ACFE. 2016. *Financial Transactions and Fraud Schemes*. http://www.acfe.com/uploadedFiles/ACFE_Website/Content/review/examreview/12-accoutning-concepts.pdf, (accessed September 13, 2018).

19. J. Ronen, and V. Yaari. 2008. *Earnings Management: Emerging Insights in Theory, Practice, and Research.* https://link.springer.com/content/pdf/10.1007%2F978-0-387-25771-6.pdf

20. PACOB. 2015. *AS 2401: Consideration of Fraud in a Financial Statement Audit.* https://pcaobus.org/Standards/Auditing/Pages/AS2401.aspx

21. AICPA. 2012. *AU-C Section 240.* https://www.aicpa.org/Research/Standards/AuditAttest/DownloadableDocuments/AU-C-00240.pdf

22. ACFE. 2011. *Introduction to Fraud Examination.* https://www.acfe.com/uploadedFiles/Shared_Content/Products/Self-Study_CPE/intro-to-fraud-exam-2011-extract.pdf

23. ACFE. 2016. *Report to the Nations on Occupational Fraud and Abuse.* http://www.acfe.com/rttn2016.aspx, (accessed March 14, 2018).

24. Ibid.

25. Ibid.

26. Ibid.

27. ACFE. 2016. *Report to the Nations.* https://www.acfe.com/rttn2016/docs/2016-report-to-the-nations.pdf, (accessed October 21, 2017).

28. ACFE. 2017. *ACFE Code of Professional Ethics.* http://www.acfe.com/uploadedFiles/ACFE_Website/Content/documents/Code-Of-Ethics.pdf, (accessed October 21, 2017).

29. Cornell. Legal Information Institute. https://www.law.cornell.edu/

30. Ibid.

31. ACFE. 2016.

32. ACCA. 2018. *Forensic Auditing.* http://www.accaglobal.com/us/en/student/exam-support-resources/professional-exams-study-resources/p7/technical-articles/forensic-accounting.html

33. Tennessee Society of CPAs (TSCPA). June, 2015. *Conducting Effective Fraud Brainstorming Sessions.* https://www.tscpa.org/docs/default-source/default-document-library/cpe_fraudbrainstorm_mayjune2015.pdf?sfvrsn=2

34. Ibid.

35. Ibid.

36. AICPA. 2002.

37. T.P. DiNapoli. n.d. *Red Flags for Fraud.* https://www.osc.state.ny.us/localgov/pubs/red_flags_fraud.pdf

38. SAS. 2017. *How It Works.* https://www.sas.com/en_us/insights/analytics/predictive-analytics.html

39. L.M. Smith. 1994. "Accounting Expert Systems," *The CPA Journal Online.* http://archives.cpajournal.com/old/16458936.htm, (accessed September 17, 2018).

40. AICIPA. 2017. *AU-C Section 520: Analytical Procedures.* https://www.aicpa.org/Research/Standards/AuditAttest/DownloadableDocuments/AU-C-00520.pdf

41. R. Kanapickiene, and Z. Grundiene. 2015. *The Model of Fraud Detection in Financial Statements by Means of Financial Ratios.* https://ac.els-cdn.com/S1877042815059005/1-s2.0-S1877042815059005-main.pdf?_tid=8312b854-0b54-11e8-a8c5-00000aab0f26&acdnat=1517932004_f34c411fb7391be5aef7c5d940699e39

42. J.C. Collins. April 1, 2017. "Using Excel and Benford's Law to Detect Fraud," *Journal of Accountancy.* https://www.journalofaccountancy.com/issues/2017/apr/excel-and-benfords-law-to-detect-fraud.html

43. Ibid.

44. R. Patidar, and L. Sharma. September 18, 2018. "Credit Card Fraud Detection Using Neural Network," *International Journal of Soft Computing and Engineering.* https://pdfs.semanticscholar.org/0419/c275f05841d87ab9a4c9767a4f997b61a50e.pdf

45. Ernst Young. 2013. *Forensic Data Analytics.* https://www.ey.com/Publication/vwLUAssets/EY_-_Forensic_Data_Analysis/$FILE/Forensics-Data-Analytics.pdf

46. Ibid.

47. C.E. Hogan, Z. Rezaee, R.A. Riley, and U.K. Velury. 2008. "Financial Statement Fraud: Insights from the Academic Literature," *AUDITING: A Journal of Practice and Theory* 27, pp. 231–52.

CHAPTER 2

Forensic Accounting Techniques

Executive Summary

Forensic accountants use accounting and auditing techniques as well as the legal rule of evidence during their investigation and the preparation of reports. Forensic accountants should assess the risk of unfavorable events that can lead to the occurrences fraud. Forensic accountants also evaluate the internal controls to ensure they are adequate and effective in responding to the related risks. This chapter presents the role of forensic accountants in risk assessment, internal control evaluation, and implementation of investigative techniques in gathering sufficient and competent evidence to support their opinions.

Introduction

Organizations of all sizes, types, and complexities are experiencing many risks that should be assessed and managed through effective risk management systems. Forensic accountants can be hired to assist management in the organization's risk management system and internal controls. Internal controls are a set of control activities designed to prevent, detect, and correct errors, irregularities, and fraud that may enter the business processes. Forensic accountants can also be hired to assist management with internal control design, implementation, and assessment. Forensic accountants can use their technical skills with their skeptical attributes in employing a risk-based approach in performing assessment of controls over their company's operational effectiveness, reliability of financial reports, and compliance with applicable laws, rules, and regulations. This chapter presents the role of forensic accountants in risk assessment, control evaluation, and investigation techniques in performing fraud and nonfraud forensic accounting services and in the preparation of their reports.

Risk Management

Business organizations are facing many risks from operational to financial, compliance, reputational, and cybersecurity. These risks, their effective assessment and management, and related internal controls affect the operational effectiveness, reliability and credibility of financial statements and compliance with applicable laws, rules, regulations and standards. Management is primarily responsible for risk assessment and management that affect business operations, compliance and the integrity and reliability of financial statements. Forensic accountants can provide assurance to the audit committee and management on the managerial process designed to manage the risks and minimize their impacts on operations, financial reporting, and performance achievements. The primary role of forensic accountants is to provide assurance on the processes designed to manage risk, implement effective internal controls, and produce reliable financial statements. Forensic accountants focus more on effective risk assessments and use a risk-based approach in their investigation coverage by: (1) identifying and assessing risk: (2) adopting a process approach to risk assessment and planning; (3) leveraging prior assessment results; (4) aligning risk assessments with management risk appetite; (5) coordinating with other risk management groups including internal and external auditors; (6) assessing the entire risk management profile of their organization, including risks related to financial reporting, operations, strategy, and information technology; (7) prioritizing risk management categories in terms of their threads to their organizations' sustainable performance; (8) working with senior management and the audit committee in the assessment process to address risks and minimize their effects; (9) establishing a risk-based internal audit plan on the basis of an enterprise-wide risk management assessment; and (10) formulating opinions and communicating findings to the audit committee, management, and other applicable stakeholders.

Forensic accountants can also conduct fraud risk assessment and management. Fraud risk management includes proper corporate governance measures (tone at the top), policies and procedures for risk identification, assessment, fraud prevention, fraud detection, and fraud investigation. Fraud risk management consists of identification and assessment of inherent risk, control risk, and detection risk in the context of the fraud triangle of incentives/pressures, opportunities, and rationalization.

Forensic accountants can use the audit risk (AR) model developed by external auditors. The goal of an auditor is to conduct the audit of financial statements in a manner that results in minimal AR. As such, Public Company Accounting Oversight Board (PCAOB) Auditing Standard (AS) No. 8, *Audit Risk,* focuses on an auditor's consideration of AR when auditing financial statements.[1]

The PCAOB AS No. 8 highlights:

- Audit risk (the risk that the auditor expresses and inappropriate audit opinion when financial statements are materially misstated)
- Risk of material misstatement (the risk that financial statements are materially misstated)
- Detection risk (the risk that procedures performed by the auditor will not detect an existing misstatement that may be material singularly or in combination)

The AR model often used by external auditors is an appropriate approach that forensic accountants can utilize in gathering evidence about fraud risk. The AR model is not intended to be a mathematical mode as certain minimum standard should apply in all situations pertaining forensic accounting services. The specification of risk model is different for forensic accountants as they investigate fraud. Forensic accountants can use the AR model to justify the means of gathering evidence sufficient, competent, and credible evidence. In the auditing literature and authoritative statements, the AR model is specified in four components as follows[2]:

$$AR = IR \times CR \times DR.$$

Audit risk (AR) is the risk that the auditor issues an inappropriate audit opinion or fails to modify the opinion on materially misstated financial statements, for example, issuing an unqualified opinion on such statements. For forensic accountants this can be defined as an "investigative risk" of making wrong investigative decision. The ultimate goal is to assess, manage and minimize this AR for external auditors or investigative risk for forensic accountants.

Inherent risk (IR) is the risk of the susceptibility of an assertion to material misstatements in the absence of proper internal controls. It is the risk that material misstatements enter the financial reporting process because of ineffective corporate governance, lack of management integrity, or relative risk relevant to individual accounts. Management is primarily responsible for managing and controlling the IR; however, the auditor's responsibility is to assess this risk and its impact on the audit plan. Given that forensic accountants are skeptical and searching for incidents of fraud, the IR is always high and, in many cases, closer to 100 percent. For forensic accountants this IR is the risk that errors, irregularities, noncompliance and fraud have occurred.

Control risk (CR) is the risk that internal controls fail to prevent, detect, and correct material misstatements caused by error, irregularities, noncompliance and fraud. Management is responsible for establishing and maintaining an adequate and effective internal control structure to prevent errors, irregularities, noncompliance and fraud on a timely basis. The auditor's responsibility is to assess the CR and determine its impact on audit planning of internal control over both financial reporting and financial statements. Forensic accountants also assess internal CR with a keen focus on that fraud and nonfraud incidents could occur and were undetected by the internal control system.

Detection risk (DR) is the risk that audit procedures fail to discover material misstatements, given that they have entered the financial reporting process and they went undetected by the internal control structure. The auditor is primarily responsible to manage and control the DR by designing and implementing an effective audit strategy. DR can be classified into analytical procedures risk, which is the risk that analytical procedures fail to detect material misstatements, and substantive tests of details risk, which is the risk that substantive tests fail to detect material misstatements that are not detected by internal controls and analytical procedures. For forensic accountants, this DR is very important as they often defend they work and decisions under the court system. Forensic accountants are responsible to assess, manage and minimize DR to the level of acceptance in the court of law.

Forensic accountants should modify the above AR model by integrating the three elements of the fraud triangle, namely pressures/incentives, opportunities, and rationalization into all three components of IR, CR, and DR. Forensic accountants should combine all three risk components with three elements of the fraud triangle. For example, forensic accountants in assessing the IR should consider fraudsters' incentives, opportunity, and rationalization. This integrated risk model for forensic accountants focuses on conventional risk elements and fraud components and should be an effective approach in assessing fraud risk. Exhibit 2.1 shows integration of fraud triangle with the risk model.

Exhibit 2.1

Fraud Risk Assessment: Integration of Risk and Fraud Components

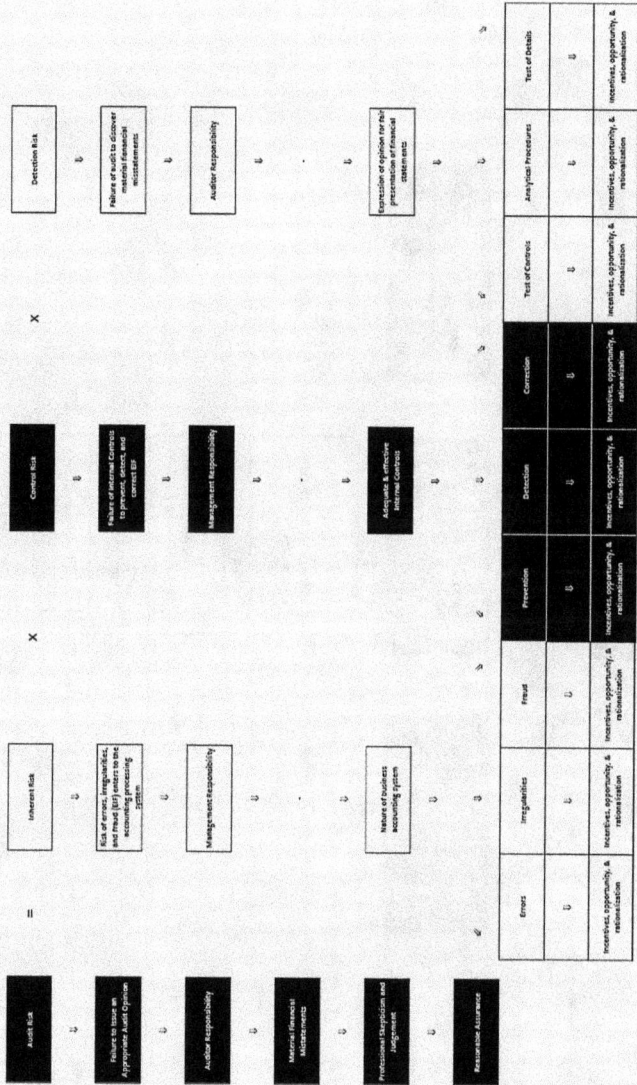

Audit Risk
↓
Failure to Issue an Appropriate Audit Opinion
↓
Auditor Responsibility
↓
Material Financial Misstatements
↓
Professional Skepticism and Judgement
↓
Reasonable Assurance

=

Inherent Risk
↓
Risk of errors, irregularities, and fraud (EIF) prior to the accounting processing system
↓
Management Responsibility
↓
Nature of business accounting system

Errors	Irregularities	Fraud
↓	↓	↓
Incentives, opportunity, & rationalization	Incentives, opportunity, & rationalization	Incentives, opportunity, & rationalization

X

Control Risk
↓
Failure of Internal Controls to prevent, detect, and correct EIF
↓
Management Responsibility
↓
Adequate & Effective Internal Controls

Prevention	Detection	Correction
↓	↓	↓
Incentives, opportunity, & rationalization	Incentives, opportunity, & rationalization	Incentives, opportunity, & rationalization

X

Detection Risk
↓
Failure of audit to discover material financial misstatements
↓
Auditor Responsibility
↓
Expression of opinion for fair presentation of financial statements

Test of Controls	Analytical Procedures	Test of Details
↓	↓	↓
Incentives, opportunity, & rationalization	Incentives, opportunity, & rationalization	Incentives, opportunity, & rationalization

(Continued)

Exhibit 2.1 (Continued)

Audit Risk Model

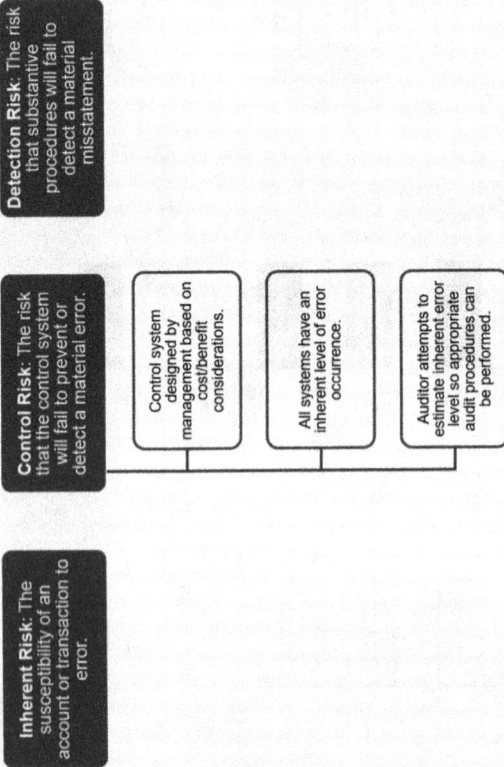

Inherent Risk: The susceptibility of an account or transaction to error.

Control Risk: The risk that the control system will fail to prevent or detect a material error.

Detection Risk: The risk that substantive procedures will fail to detect a material misstatement.

Control system designed by management based on cost/benefit considerations.

All systems have an inherent level of error occurrence.

Auditor attempts to estimate inherent error level so appropriate audit procedures can be performed.

The Committee of Sponsoring Organizations of the Treadway Commission (COSO) released its "Fraud Risk Management Guide" in September 2016, which suggests a comprehensive monitoring and assessment approach in managing fraud risk including FSF by all corporate gatekeepers from the board of directors to management, internal auditors, external auditors, and others such as forensic accountants. The guide details processes in programs that aid organizations in detecting and managing fraud risk and reduce fraud incidents.[3]

Forensic accountants should assist their client organization to implement fraud risk assessment and management consisting of the following fraud risk management components:

1. Develop an effective fraud governance process
   The development of effective fraud governance process is the first and most important step in engaging all corporate gatekeepers from the board of directors to executive and auditors. The effectiveness of corporate governance structure determines the robustness of risk assessment and management. A strong corporate governance system often includes an appropriate tone at the top and strong ethical leadership, systems of internal control, and a culture that promotes the ethical and moral over profits. These will be discussed in the next three steps.

2. Establish effective and efficient antifraud culture
   The establishment of effective and efficient antifraud policies and procedures is essential in ensuring fraud deterrence, detection, prevention, and correction. Boundaries must be set on what fraud is acceptable. For instance, the report notes that many companies have an issue distinguishing between high-level and low-level fraud, and therefore, punish them the same. After developing such a framework, the employees of the organization will be able to combat fraud effectively.[4]

3. Develop, implement, and maintain effective preventive, detective, and corrective fraud control activities. Fraud control activities must be developed in response to the assessed fraud risk. Proper control activities should be designed, effectively implemented, and compliance be demanded.

4. Implement accountability for alleged perpetrators by taking swift
action in response to allegations of fraud and fraud perpetrators.
Properly responding to fraud is equally important to detecting it.
To conduct a well-rounded forensic investigation, a balanced team
is required. This team is required to follow due care to preserve all
evidence while using it to achieve the appropriate result. The types
of evidence are discussed earlier in this chapter.[5]

Exhibit 2.2 summarizes the five fraud risk management principles suggested in the 2016 COSO report in two columns of fraud risk management components and principles. The last column presents the relevance
and implication of fraud risk management components and principles for
forensic accountants.

Exhibit 2.2
Fraud Risk Management Components and Principles

Components	Principles	Relevance to Forensic Accounting
1. Integrity and ethics 2. Board independence 3. Management oversight 4. Employees align with culture 5. Employees are responsible for actions	Control environment	High integrity and ethical standards are good practices when investigation fraudulent behavior.
1. Identify objectives 2. Risk assessment of objectives 3. Potential for fraud 4. Assess impact to internal control system	Risk assessment	Forensic accountants investigate many fraud schemes including asset misappropriation, fictitious revenues, and insider trading.
1. Align control with objectives 2. Technology to achieve objectives 3. Establish policies regarding internal control	Control activities	Corporate governance systems and principles.

Components	Principles	Relevance to Forensic Accounting
1. Select correct data to support internal control 2. Communicate information regarding internal control procedures 3. Communication with external entities about internal controls (e.g., external auditors)	Information and communication	Forensic accountants must often consult with internal control and accounting professional before and during litigation to gather sufficient evidence for trial proceedings.
1. Evaluation of internal control 2. Communicate findings pertaining to deficiencies to appropriate staff	Monitoring activities	Forensic accountants are often required to discuss findings with upper management and all individuals involved in the current litigation proceedings.

Internal Controls

Internal control is a process that provides a reasonable assurance that errors, irregularities, and fraud are prevented, detected, and corrected. Section 404 of SOX and PCAOB AS No. 2 and No. 5 encourage accountants and auditors to focus on compliance-driven controls in assisting management in the preparation of reports on internal control over financial reporting (ICFR).[6] Section 302 of SOX requires quarterly management certifications of both financial statements and financial reporting controls, whereas Section 404 requires annual management assessment of the effectiveness of the design, implementation, and operation of ICFR. Although management's responsibilities for compliance with both Sections 302 and 404 cannot be delegated or abdicated, forensic accountants can considerably assist management in fulfilling their compliance responsibilities.

Many companies, to comply with the requirements of Section 404 and AS No. 2 on management reporting on internal controls, turned to their forensic accountants for documentation of the effectiveness of both design and operation of their ICFR. Management is primarily responsible for the design, implementation, and maintenance of ICFR, and forensic accountants provide assurance and opine on internal control. Forensic accountants in assisting management with internal control assessment should maintain their objectivity and independence according to their charter and properly communicate with the audit committee. The extent of forensic accountant's involvement with Sections 302 and 404 depends on the company's accounting function, resources, funding, personnel qualifications, and considerations.

Forensic accountants are well positioned to make recommendations to management regarding the design, implementation, and maintenance of effective internal controls and expressing an opinion on internal control by: (1) developing and maintaining an internal control system that is adequate and effective in managing risks; (2) improving the efficiency and effectiveness of risk management processes and controls; (3) reviewing entity-level controls relevant to the company's integrity and ethical values, management's philosophy and operating style, organizational structure, human resources policies and procedures, competence and integrity of personnel, and assignment of authority and responsibility; (4) challenging management's decisions pertaining to internal control where appropriate; and (5) facilitating improvements in the internal control structure.

Investigative Techniques

Forensic accounting is viewed as a practice of providing fraud and non-fraud services in the areas of accounting, business, finance, management, marketing, criminology, and law by using digital forensics, technology, science, and investigation techniques. The following sections present some of the investigative techniques that are being used by forensic accountants.

Deposition and Testimony

Forensic accountants can be hired as an expert witness and/or consultants in litigation cases. Both consultants and testifying experts provide clarifying expert opinions; however, some key differences between the two exist. Consultants can be retained for their expertise and guidance in areas applicable to the case, assuming the client is able to fund the retainer fees of the consultants. Because of the nature of consultants, they are not eligible to be deposed, and thus have a high degree of confidentiality with clients. Unlike consultants, testifying experts cannot be retained and could possibly be subpoenaed for deposition. Testifying experts can provide similar services as consultants; however, their confidentiality is not as adamant as consultants because they can be legally required to provide information to the opposing counsel. Testifying experts, however, can deliver their expert testimony directly to the jury and judge, which could be advantageous in certain scenarios.[7]

Testifying experts typically provide their opinion surrounding the facts of a case in two forms, testimony and deposition. Testimony is delivered via a witness in court, in front of the judge and jury, while a deposition is provided out of court, and is typically inadmissible into court unless the party admits to an act against self-interest, subsequent testimony contradicts the deposition, or the witness is unavailable during the trial. Both testimony and deposition are communicated as a declaration of fact or solemn statement.[8] When in the process of being deposed or providing testimony, it is important to be in contact with the attorney to ensure all the necessary information is understood and documentation is possessed. It is imperative to know the full extent of facts established during a deposition, as contradicting it can destroy the individual's credibility. Often, an attorney will not ask a witness a question in which they already do not know the answer to, emphasizing the importance of in-court testimony consistent with deposition.[9]

Federal Rules of Evidence

The Federal Rules of Evidence were developed in 1975 and pertain solely to U.S. federal courts. In December 2016, the U.S. court system released an updated set of rules and was presented by the House of Representatives.[10] The University of Cornell maintains an up-to-date website regarding these rules. The Federal Rules of Evidence has a total of 11 articles.

Articles are sections of rules that are broken down categorically. For example, article IV covers relevance and article VI discuss witnesses.

In relation to forensic accounting, articles III, VI, and VII are of importance. Because of the nature of forensic practice, most cases accountants are involved are civil trials. Under article III, presumptions must be made. These presumptions include the defendant defending against the accusation and the plaintiff keeping the burden of proof. Article VI relates to witnesses. Within this article, rule 608 and rule 610 are most important to the forensic accounting profession. Similar to audit and financial accounting, forensic practitioners must be objective and impartial in the cases presented in court.

The best practices guide for forensic accountants suggest compliance with all applicable rules, regulations and standards as well as professional codes of conducts. Within rule 608, the federal government set standards for truthful action. A witness can be attacked for lack of character. This can damage the forensic accountant when called upon to present convincing evidence to the jury. Rule 610 revolves around religious beliefs. The rule states that if an individual has certain ties to religion, the evidence presented by said individual cannot be discriminated against on that basis.[11] It is also important to consider rule 801 before testifying in court, because an improper understanding of the two can destroy credibility and even dismiss the witness entirely, potentially severely damaging the position of the appointing counsel. Rule 801 defines hearsay as a statement not made while testifying in court for the express purpose of proving the truth of the matter of fact. More importantly, it provides that a statement is not hearsay if it inconsistent with previous testimony under oath. If this occurs, statements previously regarded as hearsay will be admissible into court.[12]

Aiding and Abetting

Aiding and abetting is known as asking another professional to commit a crime, and if convicted, results in the individual potentially being punished as a principal perpetrator. According to the Department of Justice (DOJ), there are four main components to this theory. First, the person being accused intended to assist in a crime. Second, the accused underlie the offense. Third, the accused aided in the offense, and fourth, that the offense was committed.[13] For instance, if an employee aids a boss in committing fraud in any way, this is considered aiding and abetting. Each of these four components is discussed in detail.

The first component, involving the accused individual, requires a committed crime to be determined before the pursuit of a verdict. Second, the accused must have acted with intent of the standalone crime or offense; in other words, the act must be punishable in and of itself as a crime. Third, the accused is required to be actively involved in perpetration of the offense. For example, if accused aided a business in fraudulent misrepresenting financial performance, this would be an example of aiding and abetting. Lastly, the offense must have been committed; otherwise a crime would have not taken place. In the prior example, the fraudulent reporting would be the crime committed.

To ultimately be convicted of aiding and abetting, the burden of proof is on the jury to find beyond a reasonable doubt that the individual in question intentionally aided and abetted the crime throughout all essential stages. Also, it must be proved beyond a reasonable doubt that the defendant was associated with the criminal venture and purposely assisted with the criminal activity with the purpose of aiding the success of the criminal act. To be associated with a criminal venture requires the defendant to share criminal intent with the principal perpetrator of the act.[14]

Conducting Effective Interviews

Many of the professional standards provide guidance for forensic accountants to conduct effective interviews. Forensic accountants need answers to questions to satisfy the requirements of the investigative plan and engagement contract; they will get those answers from various employees and those outside of the client organization. Employees who are being interviewed will often be nervous and intimidated by forensic accountants or they may try to hide relevant and important information from forensic accountants. In many cases, forensic accountants are aware of wrongdoing in advance of the interview, or they may discover during the interview that the employee is trying to hide some important information. When conducting an interview, forensic accountants should have eye contact with interviewees and observe their body language and behavior rather than simply taking notes and checking off a list. Forensic accountants should be a good listener and observer and digest things that are said and things that are not said. Forensic accountants should follow up with more questions when there are confusing answers and when questions are addressed differently.

Forensic accountants' skills and confidence with the interview process may affect the interviewees' willingness to participate in the interview process and provide candid answers. While, deceptions by interviewees are difficult to identify, skilled forensic accountants may improve the quality and quantity of the interview process. Forensic accountants can adjust the interview process on the basis of background information obtained leading into the interview. In this case, the interview is simply being conducted for affirmation or clarification of what is already known to forensic accountants. Interviewees may voluntary reveal new information, which is relevant to the case under investigation. In this case, forensic accountants should be very encouraging and receptive of receiving, analyzing, and following up on the information.

The main purpose of an interview is to gather as much of relevant and reliable information as possible to either conform the information known to forensic accountants or learn new information not previously available. The interview should be conducted in a collegial and congenial manner and not threatening to the interviewee and should start with welcoming greetings (a handshake), exchange of business cards, soft and short questions, and then proceed with harder, controversial and tough questions. The more the interviewees feel being respected and treated fairly by forensic accountants, the more likely they will be cooperative and forthcoming with information or answers. Again, forensic accountants should start with soft and nonthreatening questions, encouraging the interviewees to participate fully and truthfully in the interview process. The use of checklist is a good practice to ensure all relevant questions being asked and sufficient evidence/information being gathered. However, looking at the checklist constantly and asking questions from the checklist is not a good practice.

Forensic accountants should be proactive in asking questions and engaging and active listener, allowing the interviewee to thoroughly answer the questions without interrupting. Forensic accountants should look at the checklist toward the end by making sure all relevant questions are being asked. Forensic accountants may want to end the interview by thanking the interviewee and genuinely asking "are we missing any things" or "what else we have not discussed" or "do you have anything else to share." These open-ended questions are important parts of the interview process and often add more relevant information. The interview should end with a handshake, exchange of business cards (either at the beginning, or toward the end), and encouragement to follow up through e-mails or telephone calls.

Forensic accountants should be skeptical of possibility of deceptive behaviors on the part of interviewees. Some follow-up questions or asking similar questions in different ways enable forensic accountants to better understand and identify truth from deception. Different interrogation techniques can be used to get truthful statements from wrongdoers who may attempt to hide or lie about the truth to protect themselves or others.

Interrogation is different from interview in the sense that the main purpose of interview is obtain as much of relevant and reliable information as possible to either conform the information known to forensic accountants or learn new information, whereas interrogation often starts with an accusation or a confrontation with the employee about the wrongdoing acts or behavior. However, the interrogation process may result in an emotional denial by both truthful and untruthful individuals that attempt to defend themselves. The interrogation often relies on emotional and other pressures intended to convince and make a guilty person to admit to their wrongdoings. However, less direct and nonconfrontational interrogation method that enables the interrogator to discuss a variety of things with the subject before making any accusations can be more effective in discovery the truth.[15]

The interrogator may present exception reporting, handwriting analysis, video review, or other relevant evidence in starting the interrogation process to alleged guilty subject and encourage them to admit to the wrongdoing. It is typical that the subjects that worry about being caught have a fear of confessing to their wrongdoing that may result in embarrassment, termination, restitution, or even prosecution. Thus, interrogators should never offer clemency or make any false promises to a subject while showing empathy and understanding. The interrogator should be ready to accept and record the admission of guilt or the denial of wrong-doing at any point in the interrogation without forming an opinion or judging the wrongdoing. Best practices of interrogation suggest that the integrator should acknowledge that admission, showing genuine empathy, and be nonjudgmental. The interrogator's goal is to get the subject to admit or deny the wrongdoing and explain how and why it happened and get the whole confession out at once.

Preparing a Report

Understanding the reporting requirements and professional standards that are required aids in creating an effective, accurate, and sustainable report. There are three primary reports issued by fraud examiners—fraud examination proposals, fraud policy reports, and fraud examination report. The proposal is sent to the party in need of the examiner's expertise and includes details such as techniques to be used, fees, and a disclaimer that existing fraud might not be uncovered. The policy report identifies and describes differences between established internal controls and what occurs. The fraud examination report is the most important report of the three and will be discussed in the following paragraphs.[16]

Typically, after evidence of an occurrence of fraud has been found, the forensic accountant must analyze the evidence and present it to the appropriate individual in the form of a report. The rough draft of the report begins after all evidence has been thoroughly analyzed and observations have been derived from it. The report should explain the processes used to uncover the alleged fraud, the findings of these processes, and recommendations to prevent this issue from occurring in the future. The report itself details everything the forensic accountant does in preparing the report and its issuance. The report also is required to be presented concisely so that the average individual can comprehend its contents. This is essential because if the alleged fraud is found to be true, various parties could read or use the report (internal users, lawyers, judges, juries, attorneys, witnesses, etc.).[17]

Reports can be reported in writing or orally; however, it is important for the fraud examiner to keep documentation of the report if possible. The contents of a fraud report usually include a letter to the appropriate level of management and law enforcement, an executive summary, and various forms of supporting documentation (interviews, various company records, statements of individuals involved or with knowledge of the fraud, etc.), supporting the examiner's conclusion. The report itself is typically considered confidential, because it could lead to criminal and/or civil penalties.[18]

Conclusion

Forensic accountants in performing fraud and nonfraud services often assess risks and evaluate internal controls designed in response to the risks. Forensic accountants can also be hired to assist organizations' in their risk management and internal control systems. Internal controls are a set of control activities designed to prevent, detect, and correct errors, irregularities, and fraud that may enter the business processes. Forensic accountants can be hired to assist management with internal control design, implementation, and assessment. Forensic accountant can use their investigative techniques to assess operational effectiveness, reliability of financial reports, and compliance with applicable laws, rules, and regulations. This chapter presents risk assessment, control evaluation, and investigation techniques used by forensic accountants in performing fraud and nonfraud forensic accounting services and in the preparation of their reports.

Action Items

- Assess risks that may cause unfavorable outcomes.
- Evaluate the adequacy and effectiveness of internal control activities and processes in achieving the intended objectives.
- Use investigative techniques in gathering sufficient and competent evidence.
- Base your opinion on the evidence gathered.

Endnotes

1. PCAOB. 2010. *AS 1101: Audit Risk.* https://pcaobus.org/Standards/Auditing/Pages/AS1101.aspx

2. Z. Rezaee, and R. Riley. 2009. *Financial Statement Fraud: Prevention and Detection* (2nd ed., Hoboken, NJ: John Wiley & Sons, Inc.).

3. Committee of Sponsoring Organizations of the Treadway Commission (COSO). 2016. *Fraud Risk Management Guide*. https://www.coso.org/documents/COSO-Fraud-Risk-Management-Final-92816.pdf

4. Chartered Institute of Management Accountants. 2016. *Fraud Risk Management: A Guide to Good Practice*. http://www.cimaglobal.com/Documents/ImportedDocuments/cid_techguide_fraud_risk_management_feb09.pdf.pdf

5. Ibid.

6. Public Company Accounting Oversight Board (PCAOB). 2007. *Audit Standards (AS) No. 2: An Audit of Internal Control over Financial Reporting Performed in Conjunction with an Audit of Financial Statements*. https://pcaobus.org/Rulemaking/Docket008/2004-03-09_Release_2004-001_Release.pdfndard_2.pdf

7. M.J. Smith. 2015. *Effective Depositions and Courtroom Testimony*. http://rolfeshenry.com/Uploads/files/Effective%20Deposition%20and%20Courtroom%20Testimony.pdf

8. Cornell Law School. n.d. *Deposition*. https://www.law.cornell.edu/wex/deposition, (accessed October 2, 2018).

9. Ibid.

10. Committee on the Judiciary. December 1, 2016. *Federal Rules of Evidence*. https://judiciary.house.gov/wp-content/uploads/2013/07/Evidence2016.pdf

11. Cornell Law School. December 1, 2015. *Federal Rules of Evidence*. https://www.law.cornell.edu/rules/fre

12. Ibid.

13. United States Department of Justice. n.d. *Elements of Aiding and Abetting*. https://www.justice.gov/usam/criminal-resource-manual-2474-elements-aiding-and-abetting

14. C. Doyle, U.S. Congressional Research Service. 2014. *Aiding, Abetting, and the Like: An Overview of 18 U.S.C. 2.*. https://fas.org/sgp/crs/misc/R43769.pdf, (accessed October 2, 2018).

15. Wicklander-Zulawski & Associates. 2015. *History*. http://www.w-z.com/about-wicklander-zulawski/history/

16. ACFE. 2018. *Sample Fraud Examination Documents.* http://www
    .acfe.com/acfe-twocolumn.aspx?pageid=6764&terms=
17. ACFE. 2014. *Planning and Conducting a Fraud Examination.* https://
    www.acfe.com/uploadedFiles/Shared_Content/Products/Books_
    and_Manuals/2015%20Sample%20Chapter.pdf
18. Ibid.

CHAPTER 3

Role of Forensic Accountants in Corporate Governance and in Detecting and Preventing Fraud

Executive Summary

Forensic accountants work with various corporate governance participants including the board of directors, management, auditors, legal counsel, and law enforcement officials. Corporate governance plays an important role in improving the reliability, integrity, and quality of financial reports and ensuring that they are free from material misstatements whether caused by error or fraud. Financial scandals at the turn of the twenty-first century (e.g., Enron, WorldCom, and Global Crossing, among others) and the 2007 to 2009 global financial crisis suggest existence and persistence of financial statement fraud (FSF) and beg the questions of where corporate gatekeepers were to prevent further occurrences of FSF. Corporate gatekeepers including the board of directors, executive, internal auditors, and external auditors and forensic accountants play an important role in preventing, detecting, and correcting FSF. This chapter describes the roles and responsibilities of forensic accountants in corporate governance and in preventing, discovering, and correcting FSF.

Introduction

Forensic accountants work with many corporate governance participants, federal and state regulators, and law enforcement officials. Financial statement fraud (FSF) incidents are real, and their threats have significantly increased the uncertainty and volatility in the markets, which results in adverse effect on investor confidence worldwide. The FSF incidents prevent investors from receiving meaningful financial information to make sound investment decisions. Effective corporate governance plays an important role in addressing these incidents. Corporate governance has transformed from focusing on the agency theory of ensuring management works for the best interests of shareholders to a compliance process in the post-Sarbanes–Oxley (SOX) Act of 2002 intended to combat FSF to a business strategic imperative in recent years promoting business sustainability, corporate accountability, and social responsibility. The demand for ever-improving and effective corporate governance for business organizations is a global trend in recent years. However, the role of corporate gatekeepers and corporate governance participants in preventing and detecting FSF has not been sufficiently addressed in the literature. The 2010 Committee of Sponsoring Organizations (COSO) report emphasizes the importance of the corporate governance research and its relation to FSF.[1] This chapter presents the role of forensic accountants in corporate governance and in preventing, detecting, and correcting FSF.

Financial Statement Fraud

FSF has become daily press reports challenging the corporate governance and accountability of public companies as well as professional responsibilities and integrity of these companies' board of directors, senior executives, and auditors. FSF is defined in several authoritative standards[2] and reports[3] as a deliberate misstatement or omission of amounts or disclosures of financial statements to deceive financial statement users, including investors and creditors. The AICPA, AU Section 240, Para. 11, defines FSF "as an intentional act by one or more individuals among management, those charged with governance, employees, or third parties, involving the use of deception that results in a misstatement in financial statements that are the subject of an audit."[4] Alleged high-profile incidents of FSF, committed by large companies such as Enron, Global Crossing, Waste Management, Sunbeam, Lucent, MicroStrategy, KnowledgeWare, Raytheon, Cendant, and Rite Aid, to name just a few, have received considerable attention of the investing public, regulators, and the accounting profession. FSF has cost investors more than $100 billion during the wave of financial scandals at the turn of the twenty-first century.[5]

FSF has been one of the most dominating news cycles in the past several decades from Enron and WorldCom in 2001 to Madoff, Stanford Financials, and Satyam recently. There have been many FSF cases that have undermined the integrity and reliability of financial reports and have contributed to significant damages to reputation and economic losses. FSF has eroded investor confidence in the quality, usefulness, and reliability of financial statements. The collapse of Enron and WorldCom, among others caused by FSF, resulted in erosion of investor confidence that encouraged Congress to respond by passing the SOX Act of 2002.[6] The existence and persistence of FSF continues to contribute to the financial uncertainty and market volatility, which prevent global investors from receiving meaningful financial information to make sound investment decisions.

Incidents of FSF have continued to increase even after the passage of the SOX Act of July 2002, which was intended to combat financial fraud.[7] The 2010 Committee of Sponsoring Organizations of the Treadway Commission (COSO) report found 347 cases of FSF from 1998 to 2007 compared with 294 fraud incidents from 1987 to 1997 with an increase of 18 percent.[8,9] The COSO report indicates that key areas in which fraud occurs and the causes of fraud. Along with this increase in total cases, the dollar amount of fraud also increased across the spectrum. Misappropriation was 120 billion in 300 cases (mean of 300 million per fraudulent event) in the 2010 study compared with the 1987 to 1998 study where the mean was $25 million. These events occurred when the average revenues were 100 million and 16 million, respectively.[10]

The COSO report indicates that top management teams (e.g., chief executive officer [CEO], chief financial officer [CFO], treasurer, controller, and other top executives) were involved in 89 percent of reported cases from 1998 to 2007 compared with 83 percent in the 1987 to 1997 study. Of the top executives that were sent to trial, 20 percent were sent to jail and 60 percent were found guilty. As a result of these outcomes, it was discovered that the most common means of fraud were revenue recognition and overstatement of financial accounts, particularly assets and capitalizations. These frauds caused a decline in stock prices, loss in public trust, and often lead companies to file for bankruptcy.[11] When the company is not effective in generating sustainable performance, the management is under more pressure to manage earnings. Opportunities to engage in FSF are higher when the company is not doing well financially and unable to invest in effective corporate governance and internal controls. Emerging corporate governance reforms, securities laws, and best practices are intended to identify and minimize potential conflicts of interest, incentives, and opportunities to engage in FSF.

FSF occurs for a wide variety of reasons, including when motives combine with opportunity. Corporations' strategies to meet or exceed analysts' earnings forecasts pressure the management to achieve earnings targets. Managers are motivated or, in most cases, rewarded when their bonuses are tied to reported earnings, which can lead managers to choose accounting principles that may result in the misrepresentation of earnings. Companies are more likely to engage in FSF when quality and quantity of earnings are deteriorating, management has all incentives and pressures to manipulate earnings, opportunity to engage in FSF exist, and management can rationalize that the benefits outweigh the associated costs calculated using the probability and consequences of detection.

Economic incentives are common in FSF, even though other types of incentives such as psychotic, egocentric, or ideological motives may play a role. Pressure on management to meet analysts' earnings forecast may force management to manipulate earnings. Opportunities to engage in FSF are higher when the company is not doing well financially and unable to invest in effective corporate governance and internal controls in designing and maintaining proper antifraud policies and practices. Emerging corporate governance reforms, securities laws, and best practices are intended to identify and minimize potential conflicts of interest, incentives, and opportunities to engage in FSF. Management evaluates the opportunity for earnings manipulation and the benefit of earnings management in terms of the positive effect it will have on the company's stock price against the possible cost of consequences of engaging in FSF and the probability of detection, prosecution, and sanction.

Some of the prevailing reasons for the occurrences of FSFs are as follows:

- Poor internal controls
- Management override of internal controls

- Collusion between employees and third parties
- Collusion between employees or management
- Lack of control over management
- Poor or nonexistent corporate ethics policy
- Ineffective corporate governance

Forensic accountants' responsibilities concerning FSF are as follows:

- Consideration of fraud risks and their implications for fraud investigation
- Examination of journal entries and other material adjustments (manual, post-closing)
- Review of accounting estimates for bias—individually and in aggregate (retrospective review)
- Evaluation of the business rationale for significant unusual transactions
- Evaluation of current and prior year uncorrected misstatements
- Search for smaller misstatements over larger ones
- Evaluate employee moral
- Interviewing possible perpetrators of FSF
- Gather sufficient evidence before making a case regarding FSF
- The use of professional skepticism including a questioning mind and critical evaluation of the evidence

Forensic accountants by virtue of their independence, expertise, and knowledge are expected to discover FSF. However, they are several reasons why forensic accountants may fail to discover FSF. Among those reasons are:

- Over-reliance on *client representations*
- Lack of *awareness* or failure to recognize that an observed condition may indicate a material fraud
- Inability to connect dots
- Lack of proper attention to red flags
- Lack of *experience*
- *Personal relationships* with clients
- Not being skeptical

More specifically, forensic accountants may fail to discover FSF for the following reasons:

- Failure to exercise professional skepticism in evaluating whether fraud risk factors exist. Forensic accountants may fail to evaluate with requisite professional skepticism whether information obtained during the investigation reflects risk factors for fraud.
- Failure to gain an understanding of the client's industry and business.
- Failure to understand the rationale for and reasons behind unusual transactions. Forensic accountants may fail to adequately consider the fraud risks associated with or ascertain the business rationale for certain unusual expenses identified in company documents, including expenses incurred and earnings generated. Forensic accountants should consider the business rationale for transactions outside of the normal course of business and assess whether the rationale suggests that the transaction was entered to engage in fraudulent financial reporting or to manage earnings or to conceal the misappropriation of assets.
- Failure to appropriately respond to risk factors that arise during the course of the investigation. Forensic accountants may fail to reassess the risk of material misstatement that caused FSF, despite becoming aware of transactions and related information that warrant heightened scrutiny, including information regarding earnings management and information contrary to management representations.
- Failure to pay attention to fraud symptoms and reassess whether the red flags necessitated a change in the nature, timing, or extent of investigative procedures to obtain additional and/or more reliable audit evidence.
- Failure to conduct a thorough retrospective review of significant accounting estimates and fair value determinations. Forensic accountants may fail to perform or ensure the performance of the review process and use the performance review in assessing FSF risk. The retrospective review provides the auditor with additional information to assess whether there is possible bias in the current year's estimate.

- Forensic accountants should perform a retrospective review of significant accounting estimates and fair value estimates to assess whether there is evidence of management bias in the judgments and assumptions of fair value determinations.
- Failure to connect dots. Materiality should not be an issue for forensic accountants as any insignificant matter may lead forensic accountants toward discovery of material misstatements caused by FSF. The ability to connect right dots comes with experience and by creative and critical thinking of forensic accountants.
- Failure to pay attention to illegal acts and violations of applicable laws, rules, and regulations. When forensic accountants become aware of an illegal act in conjunction with refusal to restate the financial statements should reassess fraud risk and possibility of FSF.
- Failure to gather sufficient, competent, and credible evidence, particularly for asset valuation and ownership.
- Failure to address management assumptions for account balance estimates.
- Failure to challenge management responses to issues raised during the investigation.
- Failure to understand and have proper interpretation of U.S. generally accepted accounting principles (GAAP) and International Financial Reporting Standards.
- Failure to conduct proper and adequate investigation planning. Forensic accountant should prepare an investigation program tailored to the client's accounting and internal control systems.

Enron fraud case is presented to highlight an important role that corporate gatekeepers are playing in preventing and detecting fraud. Enron Corporation was once (2001) the seventh largest public company in the United States, and in the next year was the largest company to ever declare bankruptcy in U.S. history. In less than a year, Enron went from being considered one of the most innovative companies of the twentieth century to being the most corrupted and fraudulent company. FSF committed by Enron Corporation is estimated to cause a loss of about $70 billion in market capitalization to investors, creditors, employees, and pensioners. Its investors lost billions of dollars, directors paid penalties, executives were indicted and subsequently convicted, employees lost their job and pension investment, the auditor

(Andersen) was demised, and regulators and standard setters were blamed for not providing early warning signals of potential business failure. Enron is one example of vast FSF cases that undermine the integrity of financial reporting process and the safety, efficiency, and soundness of the financial markets.

FSF has become daily press reports challenging the corporate responsibility, accountability, and integrity of major companies as their executives (CEO and CFO) are being accused of cooking the books. Occurrences of FSF by high-profile companies have raised concerns about the integrity, transparency, and reliability of the financial reporting process and have challenged the role of corporate governance in preventing and detecting FSF. Exhibit 3.1 presents a list of high-profile cases of FSF that have proved to be detrimental to sustainability of public companies and caused risks to the efficiency and safety of the financial markets. Exhibit 3.1 reveals that common themes of reported FSF are as follows:

1. Lack of transparency and disclosures on complex financial products, including subprime loans, structured finance, off-balance sheet transactions, and credit derivatives.
2. Lack of accountability, because the financial companies were not responsible through market discipline or by regulators.
3. Lack of governance and oversight by those responsible for overseeing corporate governance, financial reporting, audit activities, and risk management.
4. Lack of effective engagement of "gatekeepers" including the board of directors, legal counsel, and internal and external auditors.
5. Lack of effective analysis by credit rating agencies.
6. Conflicts of interest and conflicting incentives for corporate directors, officers, and auditors to maximize their interests at the investors' expense.
7. Opportunities to engage in earnings manipulations and focus on short-term performance.
8. Incentive structure driven by fees and a process linked to short-term performance rather than sustainable performance.
9. Lax regulatory environment created by regulators' attempt to follow the "principles-based" regulatory process used in other countries.
10. Market discipline cannot and should not be a substitute for sound, cost-effective, and efficient regulations.

Exhibit 3.1

Reported Financial Statement Fraud

Company	Allegations	Reported Date
Adelphia Communications	Founding Rigas family collected $3.1 billion in off-balance sheet loans backed by Adelphia; overstated results by inflating capital expenses and hiding debt.	April 2002
AOL Time Warner	As the ad market faltered and AOL's purchase of Time Warner loomed, AOL inflated sales by booking barter deals and ads it sold on behalf of others as revenue to keep its growth rate up and seal the deal. AOL also boosted sales via "round-trip" deals with advertisers and suppliers.	July 2002
Arthur Andersen	Shredding documents related to audit client Enron after the SEC launched an inquiry into Enron.	November 2001
Bristol-Myers Squibb	Inflated its 2001 revenue by $1.5 billion by "channel stuffing," or forcing wholesalers to accept more inventory than they can sell to get it off the manufacturer's books.	July 2002
CMS Energy	Executing "round-trip" trades to artificially boost energy trading volume.	May 2002
Duke Energy	Engaged in 23 "round-trip" trades to boost trading volumes and revenue.	July 2002
Dynegy	Executing "round-trip" trades to artificially boost energy trading volume and cash flow.	May 2002
El Paso	Executing "round-trip" trades to artificially boost energy trading volume.	May 2002

(Continued)

Exhibit 3.1 (*Continued*)

Company	Allegations	Reported Date
Enron	Boosted profits and hid debts totaling over $1 billion by improperly using off-the-books partnerships; manipulated the Texas power market; bribed foreign governments to win contracts abroad; manipulated California energy market.	October 2001
Freddie Mac	The firm understated earnings for 2002. The fine was $125 million.	December 2002
Global Crossing	Engaged in network capacity "swaps" with other carriers to inflate revenue; shredded documents related to accounting practices.	February 2002
Halliburton	Improperly booked $100 million in annual construction cost overruns before customers agreed to pay for them.	May 2002
Homestore.com	Inflating sales by booking barter transactions as revenue.	January 2002
Kmart	Anonymous letters from people claiming to be Kmart employees allege that the company's accounting practices intended to mislead investors about its financial health.	January 2002
Merck	Recorded $12.4 billion in consumer-to-pharmacy co-payments that Merck never collected.	July 2002
Mirant	The company said it may have overstated various assets and liabilities.	July 2002
Monsanto	Improperly accounted for rebates that affected financial statements. Was fined $80 million.	February 2016

Company	Allegations	Reported Date
Nicor Energy, LLC, a joint venture between Nicor and Dynegy	Independent audit uncovered accounting problems that boosted revenue and underestimated expenses.	July 2002
Parmalat	Europe's biggest bankruptcy (around 14 billion pounds) due to falsifying accounting information. The responsible party, Calisto Tanzi, served 10 years in prison.	September 2003
Penn West Exploration	Four years of overstated profits equating to $5 billion.	July 2014
Peregrine Systems	Overstated $100 million in sales by improperly recognizing revenue from third-party resellers.	May 2002
Qwest Communications International	Inflated revenue using network capacity "swaps" and improper accounting for long-term deals.	February 2002
Reliant Energy	Engaging in "round-trip" trades to boost trading volumes and revenue.	May 2002
Toshiba	Overstated profits by 738 million pounds over a 6-year period.	July 2015
Tyco	Ex-CEO L. Dennis Kozlowski indicted for tax evasion. SEC investigating whether the company was aware of his actions, possible improper use of company funds and related-party transactions, as well as improper merger accounting practices.	May 2002
WorldCom	Overstated cash flow by booking $3.8 billion in operating expenses as capital expenses; gave founder Bernard Ebbers $400 million in off-the-books loans.	March 2002

(*Continued*)

Exhibit 3.1 (*Continued*)

Company	Allegations	Reported Date
Xerox	Falsifying financial results for 5 years, boosting income by $1.5 billion.	June 2000
Valeant	Overstated sales by $50 million.	March 2016

Source: SEC: Securities and Exchange Commission. CFTC: Commodity Futures Trading Commission. DOJ: U.S. Department of Justice. http://www.forbes.com/home/2002/07/25/accountingtracker.html

There are many reasons why FSF may occur. These reasons fall under the three categories—conditions, corporate structure, and choice (3Cs)[12]—which explain motivations, opportunities, and rationalizations for the commission of FSF. Conditions provide motivations and opportunities for perpetrators to engage in FSF. FSF will occur when the benefits to perpetrate outweigh the associated costs. Pressures on corporations to meet analysts' earnings forecasts play an important role in the commission of FSF. Management evaluates the benefits of overstating earnings and assets and/or understating liabilities and expenses in terms of a positive effect on the company's stock price against the costs and consequences of committing FSF and the probability of detection, prosecution, and sanction.

Exhibit 3.2 presents several FSF studies and cases that highlight the existence and persistence of fraud cases. Corporate structure can create an environment that increases the likelihood of the occurrence of FSF. Given that FSF is typically committed by the top management team (i.e., more than 80 percent committed by top executives, CEOs, and CFOs),[13] one would expect incidences to occur most in an environment characterized by irresponsible and ineffective corporate governance. The characteristics and attributes of the corporate governance structure, most likely to be associated with FSF, are aggressiveness, arrogance, cohesiveness, loyalty, trust, control ineffectiveness, and gamesmanship. Aggressiveness and arrogance can be signified by the company's attitude and motivations toward being the world's leading company or exceeding analysts' earnings expectations by cooking the books.

Exhibit 3.2

Summary of Recent Fraud Studies and Cases

COSO Report[a]

1. Financial pressures were important contributory factors for the commitment of financial statement fraud (FSF).

2. Top executives (e.g., CEOs and CFOs) were commonly involved in FSF.

3. The majority of alleged FSF were committed by small companies.

4. Boards of directors and audit committees of the fraud companies were weak and ineffective.

5. Adverse consequences for fraud companies were bankruptcy, significant changes in ownership, and delisting by national stock exchanges.

6. Cumulative amounts of FSF were relatively significant and large.

7. More than half of the alleged FSFs involved overstatement of revenues.

8. Most FSF were not isolated to a single fiscal period.

9. About 55% of the audit reports issued in the last year of the fraud period contained unqualified opinions.

10. Majority of the sample fraud companies (56%) were audited by a Big 8/Big5 auditing firm.

Business Fraud Survey[b]

1. Nearly 15% reported management misappropriation as the greatest fraud risk to their organization.

2. About 60% of the respondents reported their department's fraud risk analysis process as being reactive in nature.

3. The majority of respondents (72%) reported that their organizations did not have fraud detection and deterrence program in place.

4. The majority of the respondents (68%) reported that they never felt pressured to compromise the adherence to their organization's standards of ethical conduct.

5. The majority of the respondents reported their organization's external auditors as being ineffective in preventing and detecting fraud.

6. The majority of the respondents believed that more budget should be devoted to fraud-related activities and training in their internal audit department.

KPMG Survey[c]

1. Medical insurance claims fraud had the greatest average cost per incident followed by FSF.

2. FSF resulted in an average loss of $1.24 million per incident.

3. Poor internal controls and management override of controls were considered as the two most conditions for occurrence of fraud.

4. Various types of collusion were cited as important causes of fraud.

5. Personal financial pressures were considered as important red flags signaling the possibility of fraud occurrence.

6. Suggested fraud prevention and detection strategies are: effective internal controls, the tone at the top, training courses in fraud prevention and detection, a corporate code of conduct, and ethics training.

Sources in the order of presentation in the table, from left to right, are:

[a]Committee of Sponsoring Organizations of the Treadway Commission (COSO). 1999. "Fraudulent Financial Reporting; 1987-1997, an Analysis of U.S. Public Companies."

[b]The Institute of Management and Administration (IOMA) and The Institute of Internal Auditors (IIA). 1999. "Business Fraud Survey." http://www.theiia.org

[c]KPMG. 1999. "1998 Fraud Survey." http://www.kpmg.com

(Continued)

Exhibit 3.2 (*Continued*)

Ernst & Young Survey[a]

1. More than 20% of the respondents were aware of fraud in their workplace.
2. Nearly 80% would be willing to turn in a colleague thought to be committing a fraudulent act.
3. Employees lose a staggering 20% of every dollar earned to some type of workplace fraud.
4. Most frequently committed frauds are theft of office items, claiming extra hours worked, inflating expense accounts, and taking kickbacks from suppliers.
5. Women are more likely than men to report fraudulent activities.
6. Older employees were more likely to be willing to report fraudulent activities than younger employees.

Wells Fargo[b]

1. Employees became aware of an exploit in the Wells Fargo system, allowing them to open fraudulent accounts. (Opportunity)
2. A hostile work environment was created by Corporate Leadership when they aggressively raised the goals of employees and decreased incentive pay. (Pressure)
3. "Either you are moving up or moving out." Employees were afraid that they would lose their jobs. (Rationalization)
4. Internal controls were weak. The article gives the example that an employee in San Francisco and the other in Chicago could both use the same gap in internal controls to make the fake accounts.

Volkswagen[c,d]

1. The CEO and five other executives were indicted in federal court on charges of wire fraud and conspiracy.
2. The CEO himself was charged with four felony counts including:
   a. Conspiracy to defraud the United States
   b. Wire fraude.
   c. Violating the Clean Air Act
3. Employees were said to present PowerPoint slides to the CEO and other management providing an explanation as to how the software worked, thus refuting claims of ignorance.

[a]Ernst & Young. 2002. "American Works: Employers Lose 20 Percent of Every Dollar to Work Place Fraud." http://www.ey.com/global/content.nsf/us/Media_-_Release_-_-8-05-02.doc

[b]Morang, S.C. 2016. "Big Frauds," *Fraud Magazine*. http://www.fraud-magazine.com/article.aspx?id=4294994748

[c]Wolff-Mann, E. 2018. "VW Emissions Scandal," *Yahoo Finance*. https://finance.yahoo.com/news/vws-emission-scandal-goes-beyond-corporate-lies-180304829.html

[d]Shepardson, D. 2018. "Ex-Volkswagen CEO Winterkorn Charged in U.S. Over Diesel Scandal," *Yahoo Finance*. https://finance.yahoo.com/news/ex-volkswagen-ceo-winterkorn-charged-194713779.html

Source: IRS.GOV. 2018. "Examples of Corporate Fraud Investigations Fiscal Year 2017." https://www.irs.gov/compliance/criminal-investigation/examples-of-corporate-fraud-investigations-fiscal-year-2017

M.E. Zukerman & Co. (MEZCO)

1. Zukerman intended to evade income taxes by neglecting to report the sale of a petroleum products company he owned through a subsidiary.
2. The oil company sold for $130 million and corporate income taxes due amounted to $33 million.
3. Zukerman directed tax preparers to generate income tax forms for himself, his wife, and other family members that claimed millions of dollars in total in fraudulent deductions and expenses.
4. Zukerman directed corporate funds to pay for domestic employees.
5. Zukerman fraudulently claimed charitable contribution deductions totaling $1 million for the years 2009 and 2011 and then purchased 240 acres on a small island off the coast of Maine. This purchase was allegedly for conservation purposes but was instead for the benefit of himself and his family.
6. Zukerman provided false documentation and information during three separate audits to hide his actions.
7. Zukerman was sentenced to 70 months in prison, 3 years of supervised release, and ordered to pay $37,547,951 in restitution.

Nick's Roast Beef

1. Boston, MA: Nicholas Koudanis skimmed approximately $6 million in cash receipts from the business over 6 years and neglected to report this on his business or personal tax returns.
2. From 2008 to 2013 co-owners Nicholas Koudanis and Nicholas Markos skimmed over $1 million in cash receipts each year and did not report the income on their personal or corporate returns.
3. Each week the co-owners divided the cash receipts, determined how much to deposit into business accounts and report on their tax returns, how much to pay suppliers and employees, and how much to keep for themselves.
4. The bookkeeper Eleni Koudanis (wife) provided some of the false income information to their tax preparer, and their son Steven Koudanis generated the false cash register receipts used during an IRS tax audit of the business.
5. By the end of 2014, Nicholas and Eleni Koudanis accumulated $1.6 million in cash in their home safe.
6. Nicholas Koudanis was sentenced to 24 months in prison, 2 years of supervised release, and ordered to pay restitution of $2,042,366. His wife was sentenced to pay the same and given 1-year probation. His son was sentenced to 1-year house arrest and ordered to pay $151,240 to the IRS.

HBO

1. Jennifer Choi was responsible for scheduling hairstyling, wardrobe, and make-up for HBO actors. She set up a company called Shine Glossy, LLP, that she used to submit fraudulent invoices to HBO for the aforementioned services allegedly provided to the actors.
2. Through the Shine Glossy company, Choi submitted approximately 300 fraudulent invoices that led HBO to pay out approximately $940,000.
3. Choi also used a car service for herself, her family, and friends to the tune of $63,000 that she billed to HBO without authorization.
4. Choi didn't file federal income tax returns for 2011, 2013, and 2014 despite earning hundreds of thousands of dollars those years. She also greatly under-reported income when she did file for 2010, and 2012.
5. Choi was sentenced 30 months in prison and had to pay $1,285,742 in restitution.

Cohesiveness, gamesmanship, and loyalty attributes create an environment that increases the likelihood of cooking the books and subsequent cover-up attempts and decreases the probability of whistle-blowing. Trust and control ineffectiveness can cause monitoring mechanisms (e.g., oversight functions, audit functions, and internal control structure) to be less effective in preventing and detecting fraud.

FSF has been a contributing factor to the 2007 to 2009 global financial crisis, resulting in a global economic meltdown, and has threatened the efficiency, liquidity, and safety of both debt and capital markets. These financial crises have substantially increased volatility and uncertainty in financial markets and have adversely affected investor confidence and public trust worldwide. Choice provides management with the flexibility to use its discretion to either choose ethical business strategies of continuous improvements of both the quality and quantity of earnings, or to engage in illegitimate earnings management schemes of cooking the books to show earnings stability or earnings growth. Management may be motivated to engage in FSF when (1) its personal wealth is closely associated with the company's performance through profit sharing, stock-based compensation plans, and other bonuses; (2) management is willing to take personal risks for corporate benefit (e.g., risk of indictment and civil or criminal penalties); (3) opportunities for the commission of FSF are present; (4) there is a substantial internal and external pressures to either create or maximize shareholder value; and (5) the probability of FSF being detected is perceived by management to be very low.

FSF may involve the following schemes[14]:

1. Falsification, alteration, or manipulation of material financial records, supporting documents, or business transactions.
2. Material intentional omissions or misrepresentations of events, transactions, accounts, or other significant information from which financial statements are prepared.
3. Deliberate misapplication of accounting principles, policies, and procedures used to measure, recognize, report, and disclose economic events and business transactions.

4. Intentional omissions of disclosures or presentation of inadequate disclosures regarding accounting principles and policies and related financial amounts.

The Association of Certified Fraud Examiners (ACFE) estimates that business organizations lose about 5 percent of their revenues to fraud each year, which can exceed $3.5 trillion worldwide.[15] This is just the direct economic losses resulted from FSF. Other fraud costs are legal costs, increased insurance costs, loss of productivity, adverse impacts on employees' morale, customers' goodwill, suppliers' trust, and negative stock market reactions. An important indirect cost of FSF is the loss of productivity owing to dismissal of the fraudsters and their replacements. Although these indirect costs cannot possibly be estimated, these costs are typically more than the direct money and assets losses and they should be taken into consideration when assessing the consequences of FSF. Exhibit 3.3 shows a list of global FSF, their description, consequences and accountability. These FSF cases underscore the detrimental effects of global fraud and individual perpetrators and their accountability.

Corporate Governance and Fraud

Corporate governance has evolved as a central issue within regulators and public companies in the wake of recent global financial crisis. Companies have recently undergone a series of corporate governance reforms aimed at improving the effectiveness of their governance, internal controls, and financial reports. Effective corporate governance promotes accountability, improves the reliability and quality of financial information, and prevents financial reporting fraud. Poor corporate governance adversely affects the company's potential, performance, financial reports, and accountability and can pave the way for business failure and financial reporting fraud. Corporate governance measures of the oversight function assumed by the board of directors, managerial function delegated to management, internal audit function conducted by internal auditors, and external audit function performed by external auditors are vital to the quality of financial information. An increasing number of alleged FSF and earnings restatements by high-profile companies has caused lawmakers (e.g., Congress),

Exhibit 3.3

Summary of Global Financial Statement Fraud

Year	Country	Case Description	Consequences	Accountability
2001	United States	Enron hid its enormous liabilities through Special Purpose Entities (SPEs).	Shareholders lost nearly $11 billion. Enron Corporation went bankrupt and Arthur Anderson was dissolved.	Sixteen people pleaded guilty for crimes committed at the company, and five others were found guilty. Chief officers were charged with dozens of counts each of fraud and other crimes and were sentenced to years in prison.
2001	United States	Enterasys artificially inflated revenue to increase or maintain the stock price.	Shareholders lost about $1.3 billion.	The CFO was sentenced to 11 years in prison.
2002	United States	WorldCom failed to record operating expenses properly and mislabeled liabilities.	WorldCom filed for bankruptcy protection, paid a civil penalty of $2.25 billion, and previous bondholders' bonds were paid at 35.7 cents to the dollar.	Several higher-ups were indicted for securities fraud and conspiracy, and some of them faced jail time. A lawsuit was also filed against the company but was settled out of court.
2002	United States	Adelphia participated in a complex financial statement fraud and embezzlement scheme.	The company collapsed into bankruptcy in 2002 after it disclosed $2.3 billion in off-balance sheet debt.	The founders of Adelphia were charged with securities violations, five officers were indicted, and two former officers were sentenced to several years of imprisonment.
2002	United States	Bristol-Myers Squibb inflated sales by offering excessive inventory to customers.	The company restated revenues from 1999 to 2001 and settled with the U.S. DOJ and the SEC by agreeing to pay $150 million.	The former head of the Pharma group and the ex-CFO were charged with federal securities violations. The former CEO was removed from office.

2002	United States	Qwest inflated sales and former president is accused of insider trading.	The company was fined $250 million by the U.S. SEC.	Nacchio, the former president, was convicted of 19 counts of insider trading and was sentenced to 6 years in prison and heavily fined.
2002	United States	Peregrine Systems fraudulently inflated the revenue and stock price by overstating sales.	Peregrine filed for federal bankruptcy protection and eventually canceled its common stocks. Peregrine agreed to a partial settlement with the SEC.	Ten former executives, one former outside auditor, and two outside business partners of Peregrine Systems were charged.
2003	Italy	Parmalat falsified accounting documents to show a bank account with €3.95 billion to cover up losses and debts.	A fraud investigation was launched, and the company went bankrupt.	The CEO was charged with financial fraud and money laundering and was sentenced to 10 years in prison.
2003	United States	HealthSouth exaggerated company earnings to meet stockholder expectations.	The company restructured its finances and avoided Chapter 11 bankruptcy.	The former CEO was eventually charged on 30 counts and sentenced to 82 months in prison with 3 years' probation and had to pay large fines.
2005	United States	Refco hid massive losses by selling bad debts to an unnamed entity that turned out to be controlled by the chairman of Refco.	Trading of Refco's shares was halted and later delisted from New York Stock Exchange.	The former CEO pleaded guilty to 20 charges of securities fraud and other criminal charges. He was sentenced to 16 years in prison and compelled to turn over $2.4 billion in assets to the government.
2008	United States	Madoff turned his company into a Ponzi scheme and defrauded investors of billions of dollars.	It is estimated that investors lost $50 billion through the scheme, and many business and philanthropic organizations had to close at least temporarily.	Madoff pleaded guilty to 11 federal felonies, was sentenced to 150 years in prison, and was ordered to pay $170 billion in restitution. Other executives pleaded guilty to federal criminal charges and were sentenced accordingly.

(Continued)

73

Exhibit 3.3 (Continued)

Year	Country	Case Description	Consequences	Accountability
2008	France	A French trader created fraudulent transactions to gamble with the assets of the bank Société Générale.	The bank Société Générale lost approximately €4.9 billion.	The fraudster Jérôme Kerviel was charged with breach of trust and illegally accessing computers.
2008	Switzerland	A senior trader at the Swiss bank UBS faked client records and breached the bank's safeguards against high-risk trading.	The bank lost $2.3 billion and nearly collapsed and its stock price fell precipitously.	The trader was charged with financial crimes and the CEO subsequently resigned.
2009	India	Satyam systematically made fake customer records to inflate revenue and obtain fraudulent loan and advances.	Satyam's share price plummeted, the chairman resigned, and the company restated its financial records for the 2002–2008 period.	The former chairman was charged with several offences. The SEC fined Satyam and its former auditor Price Waterhouse Coopers' Indian affiliates a total of $16 million after probing the scandal.
2011	Japan	Olympus inappropriately covered losses on its investment dating to the 1990s by using value-inflated acquisitions.	Olympus' share price fell by about 75% and investigations were made into the company in the United States, Britain, and Japan.	The company's chairman and two former executives were arrested in Tokyo and served jail time. Eight executives will also take pay cuts of between 30% and 50%.
2013	Iran	Iran's largest case of bank fraud.	This case resulted in the arrest of more than 50 suspects, including some government officials.	At least 39 defendants were charged for fraudulent criminal activities, and four of them were sentenced to death.

regulators (e.g., Securities and Exchange Commission [SEC]), and the accounting profession (e.g., AICPA and Institute of Internal Auditors [IIA]) to address the role of corporate governance as well as the integrity and quality of the financial reporting process and audit efficacy.

The Enron debacle, caused by the alleged commission of FSF, has raised concerns regarding a lack of vigilant oversight function of its board of directors and audit committee in effectively overseeing Enron's financial reporting process and audit functions. Corporate governance is viewed as interactions among participants in managerial functions (e.g., management and top executives), oversight functions (e.g., the board of directors and the audit committee), audit functions (e.g., internal auditors and external auditors), monitoring functions (e.g., lawmakers, regulators, SEC, and standard setters), and user functions (e.g., investors, creditors, and employees).[16] Corporate governance framework determines the organization's corporate governance culture, structure, mechanisms, and compliance, as well as the roles and responsibilities of all corporate governance participants. The framework also determines how organizations fulfill their roles and responsibilities, as well as being held accountable through corporate reporting and assurance.

Corporate governance has garnered considerable attention in the wake of the 2007 to 2009 global financial crisis and is now emerging as a central issue for regulators and public companies. Large public companies have recently undergone a series of regulatory reforms resulting from legislation imposed by the U.S. Congress (e.g., SOX Act of 2002 and Dodd-Frank Act of 2010), new regulations from the SEC, listing standards of national stock exchanges, and best practices of investor activism. Corporate governance measures are designed to protect shareholders and other stakeholders' interests by limiting opportunistic behavior of managers who control their interests. Corporate governance measures including proper antifraud policies and practices are intended to protect investors from receiving fraudulent financial information.

One of the key responsibilities of corporate governance participants is to ensure the quality, integrity, reliability, and transparency of financial statements and provide a reasonable assurance that they are free from any misstatements caused by errors or fraud. Proper antifraud policies and practices improve the effectiveness of corporate governance and thus reliability of financial statements.

Corporate governance reforms in the past two decades are intended to improve the effectiveness of corporate governance in preventing, deterring, detecting, and correcting FSF. Corporate governance is a process affected by legislations, legal, regulatory, contractual and market-based mechanisms, measures, and reforms, as well as best practices to create sustainable shareholder value while protecting the interests of other shareholders.[17] This definition implies that there is a dispersed ownership structure, and thus the role of corporate governance measures is to protect shareholders and other stakeholders' interests by limiting opportunistic behavior and self-dealing practices of management who controls their interests. Under the U.S. dispersed ownership system, it is highly possible that management has incentives and opportunities to engage in short-term earnings management and quarterly FSF.

Corporate governance is about leadership and accountability for (1) setting a tone at the top promoting integrity and competency throughout the organization; (2) improving efficiency and effectiveness of operations to compete in the global markets; and (3) producing accurate, complete, and transparent financial and nonfinancial information. Thus, the main responsibilities of corporate governance participants and corporate gatekeepers are to ensure the quality, integrity, reliability, and transparency of financial statements in providing a reasonable assurance that they are free from material misstatements caused by errors or fraud.

Antifraud Policies and Practices

Corporate governance and its participants play an important role in designing, maintaining and implementing adequate and effective antifraud policies. These policies are intended to to protect investors from receiving fraudulent financial information. Thus, effective corporate governance in strengthening antifraud policies and practices promotes accountability, improves the reliability and quality of financial information, enhances the integrity and efficiency of the capital market, and improves investor confidence. Poor corporate governance adversely affects the company's potential, performance, financial reports, and accountability and can pave the way for business failure, fraudulent public financial information, inefficiency in capital markets, and loss of investor confidence. Proper antifraud policies and practices improve the effectiveness of corporate governance and thus reliability of financial statements. As described in Exhibit 3.4, antifraud policies and practices can prevent and detect FSF. These antifraud policies and practices are classified into preventing, detecting, and correcting corporate governance measures influenced by all corporate gatekeepers including the board of directors and the audit committee, management, internal auditors, and external auditors. The board of directors as representative of all stakeholders (investors, employees, society) has a fiduciary duty to protect their interests and ensure that their decisions (investment, employment) are not affected by misleading financial information.

The effectiveness of the board oversight function depends on directors' independence, due process, authority, resources, composition, qualifications, and accountability. Senior executives consisting of the CEO and CFO are responsible for managing the company and its resources and operations, as well as certifying the accuracy and completeness of financial reports. The effectiveness of the managerial function depends on the alignment of management's interests with those of shareholders and ensuring reliability of financial reports. Internal auditors are regarded as the first defence against fraudulent activities, providing both assurance and consulting services to the company in the areas of operational efficiency, risk management, internal controls, financial reporting, antifraud, and governance processes. External auditors are also expected to discover and report FSF. Exhibit 3.4 presents strategies, policies, and procedures in preventing, detecting, and correcting FSF.

Several strategies can be established to prevent, detect, and correct FSF. The following are the examples of these strategies: (1) establishment of a responsible corporate governance, vigilant board of directors and audit committee, diligent management, and adequate and effective internal audit functions; (2) utilization of alert, skeptical external audit function, responsible legal counsel, adequate and effective internal control

Exhibit 3.4

Financial Statement Fraud: Prevention, Detection, and Correction

Prevention

1. Uniform set of corporate governance principles
2. Vigilant board of directors
3. Vigilant audit committee
4. Diligent management
5. Adequate and effective system of internal controls
6. Independent, adequately resourced, and competently staffed internal audit function
7. Active oversight function
8. Adequate and effective management programs and controls to address strategic, operational, and financial risks

Detection

1. Adequate and effective internal control structure
2. Responsible legal counsel
3. Alert, skeptical, and independent external audit function
4. External regulatory oversight procedure
5. Independent and competent internal audit function
6. Active regulatory oversight and standard-setting bodies
7. Attentive stakeholders including investors, creditors, employees, and financial analysts

Correction
{
1. Restatement of current year's fraudulent financial statements
2. Restatement of current and prior year's fraudulent financial statements
3. Ramification of motives and opportunities contributed to the commission of financial statement fraud
4. Establishment and implementation of strategies to regain public confidence in the integrity, quality, and reliability of financial reports
5. Development and maintenance of managerial programs and controls to mitigate and exacerbate the identified strategic, operational, and financial risks
6. Reduce the complexity of accounting standards and make financial reports more transparent

Source: Rezaee, Z. 2002. "Internal Auditors' Roles in Prevention, Detection, and Correction of Financial Statement Fraud." Internal Auditing 17, no. 3, pp. 13–20.

structure, and external regulatory procedures; and (3) implementation of appropriate corporate strategies for correction of the committed FSF, elimination of the probability of its future occurrences, and restore confidence in the financial reporting process. FSF occurs when one strategy or a combination of these strategies are relaxed because of self-interest, lack of due diligence, pressure, over-reliance, or lack of dedication. The opportunity of occurrence of FSF is significantly increased when these strategies are inadequate and ineffective.

High-profile FSF incidents in recent years have raised serious concerns about the following: (1) the role of corporate governance participants and corporate gatekeepers including the board of directors and audit committees, executives, and auditors in preventing and detecting FSF; (2) integrity, competency, and ethical values of corporate gatekeepers; and (3) ineffectiveness of internal and external audit functions in detecting and reporting FSF. Incidents of FSF are harmful to companies and their gatekeepers in many ways including the following:

1. Undermining the reliability, quality, usefulness, transparency, and integrity of public financial information, which has detrimental effects on the efficiency of the financial markets.
2. Jeopardizing the integrity, quality, and objectivity of the auditing profession, which adversely affect its reputation and relevancy.
3. Diminishing the confidence of investors and public trust on financial information.
4. Resulting in substantial litigation costs as public companies and their auditors are being sued for alleged FSF.
5. Destroying careers of those engaged in FSF, such as corporate directors and officers banning of serving on the board of directors of any public companies or auditors being barred from practice of public accounting.
6. Causing bankruptcy or loss of substantial economic losses by public companies for the alleged FSF.
7. Encouraging regulatory intervention including the passage of SOX in 2002. Regulatory agencies (e.g., the SEC) considerably influence the financial reporting process and related audit functions.
8. Causing destructions in the normal operations and performance of companies for alleged FSF.
9. Raising serious doubt about the efficacy of financial statement audits and quality of audit and assurance services.[18]

Prevention and detection of FSF is the responsibility of all corporate governance participants and those involved with financial statements' supply chain. These individuals are members of the board of directors including the audit committees, management, internal auditors, external auditors, the SEC, and users of financial reports.

The existence of responsible and effective corporate governance, consisting of a vigilant and active board of directors, an effective audit committee, and adequate and effective internal audit function, discovers the intended FSF and prevents its occurrence. When FSF is prevented at this stage, the financial information will not be misleading. However, ineffective and irresponsible corporate governance, along with the gamesmanship attitude of corporate governance, would fail to prevent the deliberate FSF perpetrated by management. Management may operate in its own self-interests rather than the interests of stakeholders. Lack of adequate and effective corporate governance (e.g., internal control) may create opportunities for management to appoint the board of directors, auditors, and the audit committee and offer the monetary incentive of their continued employment. This potential for moral hazard causes a fiduciary conflict of interest in the sense that management can bend the board of directors, the audit committee, and auditors to its will. Management may act honestly but incompetently in managing the corporate affairs. This causes management to be ineffective in creating shareholder value. In this case, the board of directors should exercise its oversight authority of replacing the current management team.

The board of directors and its representative audit committee should oversee the following: (1) the integrity, quality, transparency, and reliability of the financial reporting process; (2) the adequacy and effectiveness of internal control structure in preventing, detecting, and correcting material misstatements in the financial statements; and (3) effectiveness, efficacy, and objectivity of audit functions. Enron, WorldCom, and Global Crossing debacles indicate that many boards of directors are not good caretakers. Boards are theoretically elected to act as the shareholders' eyes and ears to ensure creation of shareholder value.

Boards are elected to hire executives (e.g., top management team) and drive their performance through the carrot (higher executive compensation) and the stick (compensation cuts and termination). However, lack of due diligence by the board of directors creates opportunities for management to engage in FSF. The board of directors and audit committee of Enron are coming under sharp criticism for allowing the use of special-purpose entities (SPEs) to overstate earnings and understate liabilities. Some directors and audit committee members are even being accused of "insider trading" for making misleading statements about the company's prospects and selling more than $1 billion worth of stock during the last 3 years before the Enron crisis.

A significant portion of Enron's success was built on an elaborate foundation of smoke and mirrors with much of its success proved to be scam and resulted from questionable business practices. In 15 years, Enron grew from inception to America's seventh largest corporation, employing more than 21,000 persons in more than 40 countries. Although the fall of Enron was because of a failed business model and spin-off ventures in water, international energy brokerage, and broadband communications, Enron's demise began when investors became aware of off-balance sheet partnerships and SPEs that hid billions of dollars of losses. One of the major techniques to facilitate the deception was Enron's executives' use of more than 1,500 SPEs and partnerships to achieve off-balance sheet treatment of assets and liabilities. Some of these transactions essentially involved Enron receiving borrowed funds that were made to look like revenues, without recording liabilities on the company's balance sheet.

In many cases, Enron personnel held personal stakes in these related-party entities, reaping profits in addition to their Enron compensation. For example, Enron admitted that Andrew Fastow, Enron's CFO, earned more than $30 million from his positions in the partnerships. In 2001, Enron found itself in real trouble when, simultaneously, the business deals underlying these transactions went sour and its stock price plummeted. Debt holders began to recall the loans owing to Enron's diminished stock price, and the company found its business sustainability and accounting positions increasingly problematic to maintain. Public disclosure of diminishing liquidity, questionable management decisions, and unsustainable business practices and performance destroyed the public trust and investor confidence that Enron had established within the business community. This caused hundreds of trading partners, clients, and suppliers to suspend doing business with the company, its shareholders selling their shares, and bondholders recall their loans, which ultimately lead to its downfall.

Corporate Gatekeepers Role in FSF

The existence of responsible and effective corporate governance, consisting of a vigilant and active board of directors, an effective audit committee, responsible management, proper audits and adequate and effective internal audit function can prevent, detect and correct FSF. When FSF is prevented at this stage, the financial information will not be misleading. However, ineffective and irresponsible corporate governance, along with the gamesmanship attitude of corporate governance, would fail to prevent the deliberate FSF perpetrated by management. Management may operate in its own self-interests rather than the interests of stakeholders. Results of a survey indicates that the majority of the respondents (about 82 percent) believe that future demand for and interest in corporate governance will increase, supporting that current initiatives toward promoting corporate governance by policymakers, regulators, businesses, and educators worldwide.[19] This survey also shows that (1) financial scandals and crisis galvanize more demand for and interest in effective corporate governance; and (2) corporate governance participants and thus corporate gatekeepers should ensure the quality, integrity, reliability, and transparency of financial statements; (3) effective corporate governance promotes accountability and improves the reliability and quality of financial information; and (4) effective corporate governance reduces FSF.[20]

Antifraud Role of the Board of Directors

A vigilant board of directors that proactively oversees strategic decisions, management's plans, decisions, and actions as well as compliance with all applicable laws, rules, regulations, standards, and best practices can be very effective in achieving good governance and protecting stakeholders from receiving misleading and fraudulent financial reports. The primary responsibility of the board of directors is the appointment of the CEO and approval of the appointment of other senior executives (top management team) to run the company for the benefit of its shareholders. Boards of directors have experienced unprecedented challenges and opportunities in the post-SOX era, and some boards still struggle to find the proper balance between engaging in the strategic decisions of overseeing managerial decisions and actions and ensuring compliance with applicable laws, rules, regulations, and standards and preventing financial scandals and crises. In the aftermath of the global financial crisis of 2007 to 2009, it is expected that the boards of directors engage more proactively in the oversight function, especially in an ever-increasingly complex business environment, the governance practices, strategic priorities in dealing with global economic and political uncertainties, financial crises, fraud, and the potential risk of cybersecurity.

The boards of directors are primarily responsible to protect investor interests and ensure that they are not receiving misleading financial information that may affect their investment decisions. A survey suggests that the board of directors can effectively fulfill its fiduciary duties of ensuring published financial statements are free from material misstatements caused by errors and fraud by (1) supervising the implementation of antifraud measures, including deterrence, prevention, and detection; (2) setting a tone at the top promoting ethical and competent behavior throughout the organization; (3) assessing management performance and compensation and its relevance to fraud risk assessment; (4) overseeing the audit performed by independent auditors in discovering material financial misstatements; (5) overseeing proper design and effective implementation of antifraud policies and procedures; (6) overseeing the financial reporting and internal control processes; (7) considering feedback received from the independent auditors; and (8) including at least one financial expert in the audit committee to improve financial expertise of the committee in overseeing financial reports, internal controls, and the audit process.[21]

Improving corporate governance and enhancing reliability of financial statements are receiving significant attentions from lawmakers, regulators, the financial community, standard-setting bodies, and the accounting profession. This well-deserved attention stems from a variety of reasons, including widely publicized business failures, high-profile alleged FSF committed by big corporations, lack of vigilant oversight functions by the board of directors and audit committee, irresponsible management, inadequate governance structure, and ineffective audit functions. The increasing interest in and demand for more responsible and effective corporate governance have provided a unique and timely opportunity for the audit committee to improve its oversight function.

The corporate culture of integrity, competency, resilience, responsiveness, transparency, accountability, and value-adding philosophy can play an important role in the continuous improvements and sustainable performance and business success. Because directors' fiduciary duty and loyalty are to the shareholders, directors should set the tone at the top in promoting a healthy corporate culture and reliable financial reports free of material errors, irregularities, and fraud to protect the interests of shareholders and create shared value for all stakeholders. The main failure of Enron's directors and officers (D&O) was violation of fiduciary duty of protecting interests of shareholders and other stakeholders (e.g., employees, suppliers, customers, government, and society). During the first week of January 2001, the revelry and celebration was an Enron event when Kenneth L. Lay, longtime chairman and chief executive, said the company would take on a new mission: Enron would become "the world's greatest company."

The Enron board "waived" the company's own ethics code requirements to allow the company's officers to serve as general partner for the partnerships used as a conduit for much of its business. Directors ignored the duty of good faith and full disclosure. There is no evidence that when Enron's CEO told the employees that the stock would probably rise that he also disclosed that he was selling stock. Moreover, the employees would not have learned of the stock sale within days or weeks, as is ordinarily the case. Only the investigation surrounding Enron's bankruptcy enabled shareholders to learn of the CEO stock sell-off before February 14, 2002, which is when the sell-off would otherwise have been disclosed. Essentially, the concern with a fiduciary's appearances is on the basis of the fiduciary's implicit role in assuring that the company will observe the spirit as well as the letter of the law. The fiduciary duty is to protect stakeholders not to violate through the waiver of the company's own ethical code.

Directors are usually subject to liability exposure under state and federal law. State law imposes on directors the fiduciary duties of obedience, loyalty, good faith, and due care. Breaches of these mandatory duties can result in litigations against directors where the court determines the nature and extent of directors' liability. It is very rare that outside directors serving on board committees come under scrutiny and investigations by federal authorities for their decisions on the board. However, the three outside directors of Mercury Interactive Corp. who served on both its compensation and audit committees and signed off on the alleged illegal and intentional backdated options are under investigation by the SEC.[22] The SEC, in June 2006, advised these directors that it was considering filing a civil complaint against them regarding their involvement and approval of manipulated stock options grants.[23] It would be the first time that all the members of the compensation and audit committees could face civil charges, if the SEC decides to take further action against these directors for conduct that did not even happen in high-profile scandals of Enron and WorldCom.[24]

In the WorldCom settlement case, 12 of the company's outside directors agreed to pay $24.75 million from their personal funds; in the Enron case, 10 of the outside directors agreed to pay $13 million in personal contributions. Agreements reached for personal contributions in these two cases may have profound and unprecedented implications for and effects on the determination of future directors' personal liability. Many have argued that the existing securities litigation trend will have a chilling effect on recruiting outside directors and maintaining existing directors who face the exposure of losing personal assets.[25] The consensus is that in these two cases, the board of directors in general and outside directors, failed to effectively discharge their oversight responsibilities and acquiesced entirely to the company's CEO and thus did not prevent corporate wrongdoings. The signal sent by Enron, WorldCom, and subsequent personal contributions is that as the guardians for protecting investors' interests, directors will be held accountable and personally liable when they allow fraud and violations of securities laws to be committed by their company's management.

The Enron and WorldCom cases were rare situations of outside directors suffering liability. In both companies:

- Outside directors' oversight responsibility was not adequately fulfilled.
- Even though they were not directly engaged in fraudulent activities, they sold their shares of the company during a time when share prices were high due to the fraud.

- The potential liability cost exceeded available directors and officers (D&O) insurance.
- Outside directors were collectively wealthy.
- Plaintiffs were either motivated to force directors to disgorge profit gained from fraudulent financial activities they failed to prevent and detect or they wanted to send the clear message to outside directors that they could be held personally liable for failing to effectively discharge their oversight responsibilities.[26]

Antifraud Role of Management

The board of directors of public companies as representative of shareholders appoints the management team heading by the CEO and other members, including the CFO, controller, treasurer, and other officers to run the company. Management, under the oversight direction of the board of directors, is primarily responsible for all managerial functions, including the development and execution of corporate strategies, safeguarding resources, ensuring effective and efficient operations, promoting reliability of financial reports, and ensuring compliance with all applicable laws, rules, regulations, standards, and best practices to create long-term and sustainable shareholder value.

Management consisting of the CEO and CFO is responsible for managing the company for the best benefit of shareholders and ensuring they receive accurate, complete, and reliable financial information in making investment and voting decisions. The effective discharge of this responsibility requires management to produce reliable, transparent, and accurate financial statements free of material misstatements caused by errors and fraud. Results of a survey show that antifraud policies, procedures, and practices of management should ensure the following: (1) the adoption of a proactive approach in addressing fraud deterrence, prevention, and detection; (2) the design, implementation, and maintenance of sound financial and effective internal control systems; (3) preparation of reliable financial statements free of material misstatements caused by errors and fraud; and (4) design and implementation of effective antifraud policies and procedures.[27]

Compliance with both the spirit and the requirements of applicable rules, regulations, and laws, including legal, regulatory, and tax and accounting rules, is one of the primary responsibilities of management. The focus of the investing community and the financial markets will continue to be on a public company's financial performance; however, recently companies' social responsibility performance has also started to receive attention. Laws, rules, and regulations have recently increased significantly in response to the emerging global competition, which has reshaped financial and capital markets structure worldwide to provide adequate protections for global investors. The globalization of capital markets and the demand for investor protection in response to financial scandals worldwide (e.g., Enron, WorldCom, Parmalat, and Ahold) also require consistency and uniformity in regulatory reforms and corporate governance practices, and thus proper compliance with them.

The global competitive nature of U.S. capital markets is driven by tougher regulatory reforms in protecting investors. According to the Corporate Fraud Task Force's 2008 Report to the President, the Department of Justice charged 34 defendants during its 4-year investigation of the Enron collapse. Twenty-six of the thirty-four were former Enron employees. The CEO, Jeffrey Skilling, and the CFO, Andrew Fastow, were among those receiving prison sentences. Kenneth Lay, Chairman of the Board, was found guilty but died while awaiting an appeal opportunity. Lea Fastow, wife of Andrew Fastow, was sentenced to 1 year in prison for her role in filing tax returns that did not include some of the ill-gotten gains from her husband's schemes.

Antifraud Role of Internal Auditors

Internal auditors are the first defence against fraudulent financial activities by assisting management to achieve operational efficiency and effectiveness, proper risk management, internal controls evaluation, financial reporting certifications, and antifraud and governance policies and procedures. Results of a survey suggest that internal auditors should assist management in (1) developing and maintaining sufficient skills to identify the indicators of fraud; (2) implementing and monitoring the established antifraud policies and procedures; (3) adopting proactive approach in detecting employees' fraud and FSF; (4) using a risk-based audit methodology in assessing fraud risk; and (5) planning audits in accordance with industry standards, and where applicable, obtain audit committee (or the board of directors) approval.[28]

Internal auditors are integral parts of corporate governance and their expertise in internal control is on the front line in preventing, detecting, and correcting FSF. Internal auditors are viewed as a first-line defence against fraud because of their knowledge and understanding of internal control structure and the business environment. Internal auditors' responsibilities for detecting, investigating, and reporting FSF are stated in their standards SIAS No. 3.[29] Recently, the IIA, in its position paper presented to the U.S. Congress, states "Internal auditors, the board of directors, senior management, and external auditors are the cornerstones of the foundation on which effective corporate governance must be built."[30] The IIA also recognizes that internal auditors are an active participant in corporate governance, yet an independent observer of that process.

Internal auditors play an important role in ensuring a responsible corporate governance and a reliable financial reporting process and an effective system of internal controls by assisting their organization in (1) improving the quality, integrity, reliability, and transparency of financial information; (2) preventing, detecting, and correcting FSF; (3) assisting management to fulfill its financial reporting responsibilities; (4) ensuring the adequacy and effectiveness of internal control structure; and (5) cooperating with outside auditors to improve audit efficacy. Andersen conducted both the external and internal audits of the bankrupt Enron, which possibly created conflicts of interest that ultimately impaired Andersen's objectivity and integrity.

Internal auditors should identify red flags that signal the possibility of fraud, investigate symptoms of fraud, and report the detected fraud or its possibility of occurrence to appropriate authorities within their organization, such as top executives, the audit committee, and the board of directors. The following suggestions can enhance the active role of internal auditors in the financial reporting process, and thus, their role in preventing, detecting, and correcting FSF[31]:

1. Assist their organization to implement the 10 principles of corporation governance endorsed by the IIA.
2. Regular meetings between the chief audit executive (CAE) and the audit committee regarding the financial reporting process.

3. Establishment of a consolidated financial statement audit function consisting of the audit committee, internal auditors, external auditors, and top management team periodically assessing the quality, reliability, and integrity of financial reporting process.

4. Close cooperation and coordination of the work of external auditors with internal auditors through an integrated audit planning process consisting of the exchange of audit plans, programs, findings, and reports.

5. A requirement that internal auditors report their audit findings related to financial statement preparation, especially when there are symptoms of the possibility of FSF, to the audit committee or the board of directors.

6. Reporting to applicable regulatory agencies or even the shareholders upon failure of the audit committee to act on FSF findings of internal auditors.

7. Enhancing the status of internal auditors as a part of corporate governance through the higher-level reporting relationship, more access to the audit committee, career development plans for necessary experience, training and knowledge, and sufficient resources.

8. Assessment of the adequacy and effectiveness of the internal control structure in general and internal controls over the financial reporting process in particular.

9. Evaluation of the quality of financial reporting process, including the review of both annually and quarterly financial statements filed with the SEC and other regulatory agencies.

10. Participation with the audit committee and external auditors in reviewing management's discretionary decisions, judgment, selection, and accounting principles and practices as related to the preparation of financial statements.

11. Assessment of the risks and control environment pertaining to the financial reporting process by ensuring that financial reporting risks are identified, and related controls are adequate and effective.

12. Review of risks, policies, and procedures and controls pertaining to the quality, integrity, and reliability of financial reporting, including related-party transactions, partnerships, mergers and acquisitions, information systems risks, and off-balance sheet financial instruments.

13. Monitoring compliance with the company's code of corporate conduct to ensure that compliance with ethical policies and other related procedures promoting ethical behavior are being achieved. The tone set by management encouraging ethical behavior can be the most effective factor in contributing to the integrity and quality of the financial reporting process.

14. Continuously assessing their organization susceptibility to frauds including occupational fraud and FSF, reviewing managerial programs and controls to address such risks, and ensuring that the established programs and controls are adequate and effective in mitigating or exacerbating the identified fraud risks.

A close working relationship between the audit committee and internal auditors can improve the effectiveness of corporate governance. First, the independence and objectivity of internal auditors can be strengthened when they report their findings and opinions directly to the audit committee. Second, the prestige and status of internal auditors can be enhanced when they work with management at all levels while being accountable to the audit committees. Third, internal auditors can be of a significant assistance to audit committees to effectively fulfill their oversight duties in functions such as financial reporting, internal controls, risk management, external audit, whistle-blowing, ethics, and taxes.

Internal auditors' reports should (1) disclose all relevant information about the effectiveness of the organization's corporate governance; (2) focus on its sustainability performance in all areas of economic and financial, social, ethical, governance, and environmental activities; (3) provide transparent financial and nonfinancial information on key performance indicators (KPIs) and their impacts on all stakeholders; and (4) assess the organization's responsiveness to the needs of all of its stakeholders.

Antifraud Role of External Auditors

FSF has been and continues to be the focus of the auditing profession. During the 1890s, external auditors viewed the detection of fraud, in general, and FSF as the primary purpose of the financial audit. The auditing profession had moved from acceptance of fraud detection as a primary purpose to the expression of an opinion on fair presentation of financial statements during the twentieth century. The accounting profession has initially addressed the external auditor's responsibility for FSF detection in SAS No. 82 and SAS No. 99 titled *Consideration of Fraud in a Financial Statement Audit.*[32] SAS No. 82, which is superseded by SAS No. 99, required the independent auditor to consider a broad range of fraud risk factors in assessing the risk of occurrences of FSF and to use this assessment in audit planning to detect fraud.

The Auditing Standards Board (ASB) of the AICPA, by issuing SAS No. 99, attempts to clarify, but not to expand, the auditor's responsibility to detect and report FSF. SAS No. 99 states "The auditor has a responsibility to plan and perform the audit to obtain **reasonable assurance** about whether the financial statements are **free of material misstatement,** whether caused by **error or fraud** (emphasis added)."[33] SAS No. 99 makes it clear that the auditor's responsibility for detecting fraud is framed by the concepts of reasonable, but not absolute, assurance and materiality and subject to cost/benefit decisions inherent in the audit process. However, although auditors are not expected to detect all employees' frauds, the public expects auditors to detect material FSF perpetrated by management with the purpose of misleading investors and creditors. Independent auditors provide reasonable assurance that financial statements are not materially misstated, and therefore, they are free of material errors, irregularities, and fraud. This level of assurance is given in an audit report on the basis of an audit of financial statements.

SAS No. 99 states that "absolute assurance is not attainable and thus even a properly planned and performed audit may not detect a material misstatement resulting from fraud."[34] SAS No. 99 requires auditors to (1) approach every audit with professional skepticism; (2) discuss among the audit team members regarding the risks of material misstatement caused by fraud; (3) identify fraud risk and management incentives, opportunities, and ability to rationalize occurrence of fraud; and (4) design audit tests responsive to the risks of fraud. SAS No. 99 requires that auditors place an increased emphasis on discovering FSF.

Although SAS No. 99 is not suggesting any changes to the auditor's current responsibilities for detecting fraud in a financial statement, it provides new guidelines, concepts, and requirements to aid auditors in fulfilling those responsibilities.

These guidelines

1. describe fraud and its characteristics;
2. discuss the need for auditors to exercise professional skepticism in conducting financial audits;
3. require auditors to discuss among the audit team members regarding the risks of material misstatement caused by fraud;
4. require auditors to obtain competent and sufficient evidence to identify risks of material misstatement caused by fraud through inquiring of management, performing analytical procedures, and considering fraud risk factors;
5. identify fraud risk factors and assess these risk factors by considering the client's programs and controls;
6. require auditors to respond to the results of the risk assessment by:
   a. determining its overall effect on how the audit is conducted;
   b. considering its impact on the nature, timing, and extent of the auditing procedures to be performed; and
   c. performing certain procedures (e.g., examining journal entries and other adjustments, reviewing accounting estimates and unusual transactions) to further address the likelihood of occurrence of fraud involving management override of controls;
7. require auditors to evaluate audit evidence indicating the likelihood of financial misstatements caused by fraud and their implications for fair presentation of financial statements;
8. provide guidance regarding auditors' communicates about fraud to management, the audit committee, and others; and
9. describe appropriate documentations of auditors' consideration of fraud.

The 2010 inspection reports of the Public Company Accounting Oversight Board (PCAOB) indicate that audit failures of detecting financial misstatements including FSF have contributed to 2007 to 2008 financial crisis.[35] External auditors failed to perform their gatekeeping responsibility of protecting investors from receiving misleading financial reports by (1) not challenging the assumptions of valuation models used in estimating fair value assets; (2) not considering risk assessment of off-balance sheet transactions; and (3) not providing early signal of financial difficulties and going concern.[36] Auditing standards (SAS Nos 88 and 99, 2002) define independent auditor responsibility in rendering an unqualified opinion is to express *reasonable assurance* that the audited financial statements are free from material misstatements, whether caused by error or fraud. Results of a survey indicate that external auditors can reduce the likelihood of FSF by (1) performing risk-based audit tests; (2) discussing FSF with the board, audit committee, and management; (3) integrating fraud risk into audit strategies, plans, and procedures; and (4) performing forensic and investigative audit procedures to detect FSF when there is likelihood of allegation of fraud. External auditors main concern is with material misstatements in the audited financial statements by reducing the information risk of be misleading and fraudulent.

Enron's collapse and related audit failures caused loss of reputation, trust, and confidence in Big 5 accounting firm, Andersen, LLP. News about charges of inappropriate destruction of documents at the Andersen office in Houston, which housed the Enron audit and the subsequent unprecedented federal indictment, resulted in the demise of Andersen. Andersen's clients quickly lost confidence in the auditing firm, and by June 2002, more than 400 of its largest clients had fired the firm as their auditor, leading to the sale or desertion of various pieces of Andersen's U.S. and international practices. On June 15th, a federal jury in Houston convicted Andersen on a felony count of obstructing the SEC's investigation into Enron's collapse. Although the Supreme Court later overturned the decision in May 2005, the reversal came nearly 3 years after Andersen was essentially out of business. Shortly, after the June 15, 2002 verdict, Andersen announced it would cease auditing publicly owned clients by August 31. Therefore, like Enron, in less than a year Andersen went from being one of the world's largest and most respected auditing firms into oblivion.

Andersen was regarded as the watchdog and moral voice of the auditing profession in the United States for many years before its demise in 2002, caused by the conviction of obstruction of justice. Although later the Supreme Court overturned Andersen's initial U.S. District court conviction, it did not help Andersen to retain its severely damaged reputation. The Supreme Court decision did not save Andersen and did not change the perception that Andersen "was a victim of its own self-indulgence." Nonetheless, a series of audit failures of Sunbeam, Waste Management, and Enron, among others, were devastating to investors and caused the public distrust of Andersen as it paid more than 500 million between 1997 and 2001 to settle claims of audit failures, looking the other way, and not reporting the discovered FSF.

Auditors must be skeptical, alert, professional, inquisitive, and understand the public trust in their profession and why they are licensed to serve as auditors. Their role is to lend credibility to published financial statements and provide reasonable assurance that financial statements fairly reflect underlying business realities, substance, financial conditions, and results of operations. SAS No. 99 defines skepticism as

> an attitude that includes a questioning mind and a critical assessment of audit evidence. The auditor should conduct the engagement with a questioning mind that recognizes the possibility that a material misstatement due to fraud could be present, regardless of any past experiences with the entity and regardless of the auditor's belief about management's honesty and integrity.[37]

Every publicly traded company has a right to be audited under the law. However, an audit is not an entitlement for receiving a clean or unqualified audit opinion. Some companies should not receive standard unqualified opinions until they clean up their act by providing objective, high-quality, reliable, and transparent financial statements. Auditors must be alert to management overriding controls, resulting in fraudulent financial reporting and misappropriation of assets.

The following suggestions can help the accounting profession to narrow the expectation gap:

1. Existing auditing standards require auditors to provide reasonable assurance that financial statements are free from material misstatements, whether caused by errors or fraud. This level of reasonable assurance is not well defined and means different things to different people. Investors view reasonable assurance as a high-level assurance and wish to hold auditors responsible for all errors, irregularities, and

fraud threatening the integrity of financial statements. Auditors, on the other hand, in recognizing the limitation of financial audits (e.g., management override, test basis, and use of estimates), can only provide a reasonable assurance which is less than absolute assurance. The accounting profession should clearly define what constitutes "reasonable assurance" in order to narrow the perceived expectation gap.

2. Given the credibility issues and expectation gap facing the accounting profession, it is important that investors have confidence in regulators (SEC) and standard-setters (the PCAOB and AICPA) in protecting investors from receiving misleading financial statements. The AICPA, the leading advocate for the view of CPAs and the PCAOB, the watchdog of the accounting profession, should be more active in addressing the perceived trust gap and ways to narrow this gap. Only more training in forensic techniques can bridge this credibility gap.

3. The accounting profession should promote the use of an integrated audit for all entities, public and private companies, and for profit and not-for-profit organizations. An integrated audit approach is the audit of both internal control over financial reporting and financial statements. Under an integrated audit, auditors test the adequacy and effectiveness of the design and operation of internal controls as well as audit of financial statements. An effective and efficient integrated audit can improve integrity, reliability, quality, and transparency of financial statements.

4. Participation in local community activities, especially activities of colleges and universities. Public accounting firms of all sizes (Big 4 and non-Big 4) should get more engaged in the development of the accounting curriculum with a keen focus on antifraud and forensic accounting.

5. Expansion of auditing and accounting services to clients assist them to ensure the integrity and reliability of their financial reports. Examples of these services are antifraud training for management, boards of directors, and audit committees.

Reasons auditors fail to detect FSF are as follows:

- Over-reliance on client representations
- Lack of awareness or failure to recognize that an observed condition may indicate a material fraud

- Lack of experience
- Personal relationships with clients
- Insufficient professional skepticisms
- Inadequate use of IT and data analytics
- Lack of focus on FSF discovery

Short Sellers Role in Discovering Fraud

Short sellers as sophisticated investors and in looking after their investments also act as gatekeepers in preventing, detecting, and correcting irregularities, and errors and fraud. However, auditors' efficacy and incentives in discovering and reporting FSF may be different from those of short sellers in the sense that auditors are concerned with fair presentation of financial statements and provide reasonable assurance that these statements are free from material misstatements, whether caused by errors or fraud, whereas short sellers search for financial challenges that influence short interest. Short sellers, through their private search and information processing skill, can identify firms with financial challenges and take actions before public disclosure of such information, and thus public disclosure of such challenges has no value relevant to short sellers. Short sellers tend to target firms with financial challenges, including irregularities, red flags of financial reporting fraud, and reported material weaknesses in their internal controls, top executive resignations, and auditor changes, and can obtain information faster than other traders before such information is publicly disclosed and reflected in stock prices.[38] Short sellers play an important role in the financial market and their incentives in targeting firms with financial challenges, including misstatements caused by fraud.

Forensic Accountants Role in Discovering Fraud

Forensic accountants combine accounting knowledge with investigative skills. Using this skill set, forensic accountants lend litigation support and conduct investigations in accounting settings. They are responsible for performing forensic research to trace funds and identify assets for recovery, conducting forensic analysis of financial data, and preparing forensic accounting reports from any financial findings.[39] Forensic accountants are responsible for finding a resolution for fraud allegations. This means performing a myriad of tasks including aiding in the prevention and detection of white-collar crime, collecting evidence (physical and verbal testimony), writing reports, and testifying to their findings.[40] Because of the important role the forensic accountants play, their knowledge base includes white-collar crime, money laundering, insurance claims, GAAP or generally accepted auditing standards (GAAS) violations, telemarketing fraud, check kiting, contract and procurement fraud, asset misappropriation, securities fraud, FSF, bankruptcy fraud, credit card fraud, embezzlement, financial data analysis, evidence integrity analysis, computer application design, damage assessment, tracing illicit funds, locating hidden assets, due diligence reviews, forensic intelligence gathering, accounting procedures, legal system and its procedures, regression analysis, and computer applications. They must possess the skill to write reports of high import as well as reliably testify as an expert witness, and their abilities must include interpersonal communication verbal communication, written communication, and attention to detail, analytical, integrity, objectivity, independence, and credibility.[41] The common ways forensic Accountants assist business organizations in performing forensic accounting services are:

1. Assist managers and audit committee (board of directors) with the aspect of deterrence, prevention, and detection processes (i.e., directly or through the participation with internal or independent auditors)
2. Provide input into management's assessment of fraud risk
3. Help to cultivate an appropriate antifraud environment
4. Assist the audit committee and board assesses susceptibility to management override and collusion
5. Resolve allegations or suspicions of fraud

Certified Fraud Examiners passing the CFE Examination requires expert knowledge of fraudulent financial transactions, legal elements of fraud, fraud investigation, and criminology and ethics. In the investigation step of the fraud examination process, individuals working in the public and private sectors are key. Public-sector investigators work at the federal, state, or local level as police detectives, federal special agents, and anything in-between. Private-sector investigators work in the field of loss prevention, internal or external fraud analysis, and as independent or agency private investigations.

Specific job positions for the public sector include state and local police, police detective, crime scene investigator, district attorney investigator, attorney general, state bureau of investigation, Security and Exchange Commission, Homeland Security, U.S. Immigration and Customs Enforcement (ICE), Transportation Security Administration (TSA), U.S. Customs and Border Protection (CBP), Department of Justice, Federal Bureau of Investigation (FBI), Criminal Division, Civil Division, Central Intelligence Agency (CIA), Bureau of Alcohol Tobacco and Firearms (ATF), and the Drug Enforcement Administration (DEA).

The knowledge required of a public-sector investigator is white-collar crime, organized crime, financial crime, bribery and corruption, money laundering, counterfeiting, fraudulent documents, and credit card fraud. Much like a forensic accountant, an investigator should be proficient in the skills of writing reports and testifying in court, but they must also conduct surveillance, collect evidence, conduct interviews, record examination, and utilize computers. Important abilities required of public-sector investigators are attention to detail, ability to function in stressful situations, alert to surroundings, understanding of associated risks, honesty, sound judgment, integrity, responsibility, fairness, compassion, leadership, accountability, and adaptability.[42]

Specific job positions for private-sector investigators include loss prevention, private investigator, internal fraud analyst, and external fraud analyst. The knowledge required of a public-sector investigator is the same as that of the public-sector accounting along with the addition of loss prevention and counterfeiting. They must have the skills to conduct surveillance, collect evidence, conduct interviews, record examination, writing reports, and utilize computers. The abilities required of private-sector investigators are attention to detail, functioning in stressful situations, being alert to surroundings, understanding associated risks, honesty, having sound judgment, high integrity, being responsible, and a having a strong judge of character.[43]

Antifraud Role of Market, Regulators, and Standard Setters

Limitations in GAAP are at least partly to blame for Enron executives' ability to hide debt, keeping it off the company's financial statements. These technical accounting standards lay out specific "bright-line" rules that read much like the tax or criminal law codes. Some observers of the profession argue that by attempting to outline every accounting situation in detail, standard-setters are trying to create a specific decision model for every imaginable situation. However, very specific rules create an opportunity for clever lawyers, investment bankers, and accountants to create entities and transactions that circumvent the intent of the rules while still conforming to the "letter of the law." SPEs were never intended to provide safe harbor to keep assets and liabilities out of a company's accounting records. In contract, for an SPE's assets and liabilities to be treated as "off-balance sheet," Enron needed to maintain at least a 3 percent ownership in the SPE and the remaining debt, and equity investors needed to have their investment capital at risk.

Enron structured the transactions so that it virtually guaranteed the investors' positions. As such, the SPE and its related assets and liabilities should have been consolidated as part of Enron. Because the SPEs were not consolidated, Enron's risk remained hidden by a veil of deception in the form of the SPEs. When Enron's guarantees came to light during 2001, the market's trust in Enron's ability to deliver as a market maker evaporated. Even more interesting was that Enron executives had significant financial stakes in some of these SPEs and personally reaped huge income from that ownership. For example, Michael Kopper, a Fastow assistant, is reported to have made at least $12 million and Andrew Fastow, CFO, more than $30 million on their related party investments in Enron off-balance sheet entities.

Enron created four SPEs in 2000. As part of the initial capitalization of these SPEs and a series of ongoing transactions, Enron issued its own common stock in exchange for notes receivable. At the time, Enron increased notes receivable (an asset) and shareholders' equity to reflect these transactions. However, GAAP generally requires that notes receivable arising from transactions involving a company's capital stock be presented as deductions from stockholders' equity and not as assets. Enron has indicated that they overstated both total assets and shareholders' equity by $172 million owing to a transaction first reported in the financial statements for the quarter ended June 30, 2000, and by an additional $828 million owing to a transaction first reported in the quarter ended March 31, 2001. Even with these accounting mistreatments, Enron was demonstrating signs of impending financial troubles. In the first and second quarter of 2001, Enron reported negative cash flows from operations in contrast to reporting operating earnings. Regulations and standards that are cost-effective, efficient, proactive, and scalable provide framework and guidelines for business organizations in developing sound business and accounting systems to prevent, detect, and correct FSF, and proper guidelines for forensic accountants and auditors to discover and report FSF.

Market Correction Mechanisms

Market can play an important role in preventing and detecting FSF by demanding full and fair disclosure of financial information of the listed public companies. Financial analysts, following public companies for compliance with listing standards pertaining to full and fair disclosures and revealing non-compliance, can cause a substantial reduction in stock prices. Any market correction mechanism for disclosure of fraudulent activities can be detrimental to companies. The capital market can monitor and punish fraud-prone companies through negative stock reactions to fraud disclosures. These negative stock reactions usually get the attention of the board of directors in replacing management and establishing effective corporate governance measures to correct fraud. However, in many fraud cases including the Enron case, by the time that the market reacts to undisclosed and disclosed frauds, these fraud companies are already bankrupt or on their way to becoming insolvent.

Academic studies, by using "fraud-on-the-market theory," find that on average stock prices are negatively affected by the disclosure of FSF.[44] The question is whether the market price is fraudulently being distorted, suggesting that stock prices are different from what they would have been in the absence of such disclosure. The fraud-on-the-market theory suggests that in an efficient market, stock prices reflect all available public information including misstatements caused by FSF, presumably at the disclosure time of FSF. However, the securities market may not be aware of occurrences of FSF before public disclosure, and thus their effects are not embedded in stock prices. It is also possible that stock prices are distorted by disclosures of FSF. A combination of the fraud-on-the-market theory and the bad news concealing theory derived from the agency problem suggests that there is an information asymmetry between management and shareholders that can motivate management to engage in FSF that may affect stock prices According to the fraud-on-the-market theory, the stock price reflects all information, including the misstatement caused by fraud. Therefore, if an investor can show that the purchased stock was priced much higher because the market price did not reflect the fraud when the fraud was not disclosed to the market, the investor has the grounds for a class-action lawsuit.[45]

There is nothing wrong with markets failing to fulfill their task of leveling the playing field between buyer and seller. Such market failures are in fact how many entities make their money through patents (temporary monopolies) and the use of expertise that is not universally available (competitive advantage). Nonetheless, the types of market failures that ignore the rights of others and endanger the credibility of all legitimate transactions have detrimental effects on business and market sustainability. The most common form of market failure is information asymmetries known to business decision makers (management) and not properly disclosed to investors. Thus, this unfairness information asymmetry exceeds simple competitive advantage and is a threat to the rights of investors and to the effective functioning of the free market system. An obvious example of this market failure is the use of "off-balance sheet," SPEs, and other related party entities by Enron with the intention to hide liabilities and exaggerate earnings. When an entity acts as a market marker, optimally, the market maker has no ownership positions in the assets and liabilities being traded; instead, the market maker assists willing buyers and willing sellers meet in an effective, efficient, and low-cost manner. The trouble with Enron was that in many of its markets, it was a counterparty to the transaction. Enron's inventory of energy and other assets also created enormous debt. Enron used about five hundred SPEs and thousands of questionable partnerships for the structure transactions to achieve off-balance sheet treatment of assets and liabilities. Enron used

SPEs to borrow directly from outside lenders, often supplying its own credit and stock guarantees. When outside investors became suspicious of the value of the SPEs, Enron offered its own stock as collateral.

In the natural gas market, Enron provided and charged for stability, marketing stable financial contracts to its customer by combining of options, swap, and similar financial instruments. The problem at Enron was that many of their contracts were custom and did not have a ready market. Custom contracts without a market are difficult to value. The alternative was that Enron valued these contracts through computer models, a process known as mark-to-model. The immediate advantage is that Enron could put a positive spin on its earnings. But the end result was: Enron not only started to believe that mark-to-model earnings were real, but also "manipulated the models to its advantage." The capital market is expected to discipline underperformed and unethical companies through extensive sales of shares of these companies and lack of investor confidence that causes substantial declines in stock prices. Exhibit 3.5 shows Enron's stock decline during the Enron debacle in 2001.

Antifraud Role of Regulators

The SECs have several divisions related to fraud and regulatory enforcement. Under the purview of the Financial Reporting and Audit Task Force, the team investigates violations related to financial information

Exhibit 3.5

Enron 2001 Stock Price

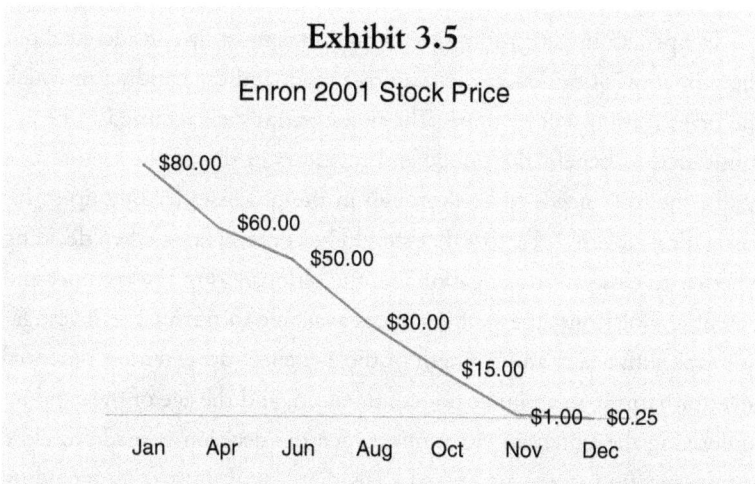

and disclosure. The SEC's Financial Reporting and Audit Task Force is also responsible for fraud detection through use of real-time analysis, running systems designed to detect fraud, and using experts to pinpoint and properly address fraudulent behavior. This task force communicates its findings with several offices, including the Chief Accountant, Economic and Risk Analysis, and Corporate Finance.[46]

The Microcap Fraud Task Force, created in 2010, joined several different operations in the enforcement and examined functions of the SEC. Research and investigative techniques are used on only microcap securities. Microcap securities have a capitalization value between $50 and $300 million. As a result, the task force is concerned about a specific set of actions, people, and firms and develops strategies on the basis of this optic. Elisha Frank and Michael Paley are currently in charge of this task force.[47]

The previously mentioned task forces were created to discover fraud. The SEC uses these groups to find fraud, but there is a general process that the agency follows. An investigation is opened first, then proceedings occur, and then finally is investigated, enforced and then closed. When opening an investigation, the SEC has two methodologies to choose from. The first method occurs when a Matters Under Inquiry (MUI) is translated into an investigation. When a MUI becomes investigative, the SEC has determined that a MUI is no longer applicable given the conclusions of the analysis. Second, an investigation may be opened when no MUI is present.[48]

To open an investigation, several questions must be considered about the validation of evidence, the resources used, and the conduct in which the investigation will be done. The investigations are required to be administered to benefit the public and investors in the public sector. As a result, the SEC needs to be thorough in the processes leading up to investigation closure.[49] Factors that should be contemplated when deciding whether to close an investigation are: the seriousness of the conduct and potential violations, the staff resources available to pursue the investigation, the sufficiency and strength of the evidence, the extent of potential investor harm if an action is not commenced, and the age of the conduct underlying the potential violations. Once the decision is made to close an investigation, there are several steps that a staff must take, including checking with the Freedom of Information Act Office (for instructions of retention and disposition of case files), preparing a closing recommendation, preparing the files for disposition, and generating and sending the proper termination notices. However, should a case result in enforcement action, it can't be closed until all enforcement actions in the case are completed. This mandates a final judgment/commission order and that all ordered monetary relief be accounted for.[50]

SEC enforcement actions are taken against firms that are identified as having violated the financial reporting requirements of the Securities Exchange Act of 1934. The SEC Enforcement Manual provides guidance to employees about the handling of complaints, tips, and referrals (leads) received concerning violations of SEC requirements. The SEC obtains leads for investigation from several sources: (1) public complaints and tips; (2) the reporting requirements of federal, state, and local law enforcement agencies under the Bank Secrecy Act; (3) the enforcement staff of the Public Company Accounting Oversight Board; (4) the enforcement of "blue sky laws" by state securities regulators; (5) complaints and other information from members of Congress on behalf of constituents whom they represent; and (6) trading-related referrals from domestic self-regulatory organizations (SROs).[51]

Antifraud Education

Effective antifraud policies and programs should be designed to prevent and detect fraud. Antifraud programs should deter, prevent, and detect all variations of fraud, from misrepresenting financial information to misappropriating assets and employee fraud. Effective antifraud programs should also address the antifraud role of corporate governance participants. Entities of all sizes are susceptible to both employee fraud (e.g., theft and embezzlement) and management fraud (e.g., manipulation of financial reports). Effective antifraud programs—focusing on fraud awareness and education in the workplace environment, whistle-blowing policies and procedures of encouraging and protecting employees to report suspicious behavior, adequate internal control procedures designed to prevent and detect fraud, and conducting surprise audits—can significantly reduce fraud.

The demand for and interest in ethics and corporate governance and antifraud practice and education has significantly increased in the post-SOX era. Ethics and corporate governance have transformed from a compliance process to a business strategic imperative—yet, many have expressed concern over the corporate governance and ethics education, as well as the training provided in an effective antifraud program. Antifraud policies and programs should address corporate culture, control structure, and fraud procedures.

1. Corporate culture: Corporate culture should create an environment that sets an appropriate tone at the top that promotes ethical behavior and reinforces antifraud conduct, demanding "doing the right thing always." The corporate culture provides incentives for everyone in the company, from directors to officers and employees, to act competently and ethically.
2. Control structure: An effective control structure should eliminate opportunities for individuals to engage in fraudulent activities. Section 404 of SOX, SEC rules, and PCAOB AS No. 5 all underscore the importance of internal controls in the prevention and detection of fraud.
3. Antifraud procedures: Adequate fraud-related procedures should be developed and performed to ensure prevention and detection of potential fraud.

Conclusion

Entities of all sizes and types are susceptible to both employee (e.g., theft and embezzlement) and management fraud (e.g., manipulating financial reports). Effective antifraud programs and procedures should be designed to prevent and detect fraud. Antifraud programs should deter, prevent, and detect all variations of fraud, from misrepresenting financial information to misappropriating assets and employee fraud. Effective antifraud programs should address the role of corporate governance participants including the board of directors, executives and auditors in preventing and detecting fraud. This chapter provides insights on the role of corporate governance participants in antifraud policies and procedures. Corporate culture should create an environment that sets an appropriate tone at the top, promoting ethical behavior, reinforcing antifraud conduct, and demanding "doing the right thing always." It provides incentives for everyone in the company to act ethically. Control structure should eliminate opportunities for individuals to engage in fraudulent activities. Antifraud procedures are necessary to ensure prevention and detection of potential fraud.

The collapse of Enron, WorldCom, and Global Crossing, among others, caused by the alleged FSF has encouraged organizations to place more emphasis on corporate governances, information systems, and internal control in generating online and real-time, reliable, relevant, and transparent financial information. The internal audit function is an important component of corporate governance and the first line of defence against FSF. The three-factor model consisting of conditions, corporate structure, and choice discussed in this chapter should assist internal auditors and forensic accountants to identify symptoms and red flags that may indicate the occurrence of FSF, assess the identified symptoms and opportunities, and notify the appropriate authorities within their organization for investigation of the possibility of FSF.

FSF occurs when one or a combination of antifraud strategies presented in this chapter are relaxed owing to self-interest, lack of due diligence, pressure, over-reliance, or lack of dedication. The opportunity of occurrence of FSF is significantly increased when antifraud strategies are inadequate and ineffective. The opportunity to engage in FSF increases as the organization's control structure weakens, its corporate governance becomes ineffective, and its audit efficacy deteriorates. One important lesson learned from Enron's collapse is the relevance and importance of a proactive, responsible, and vigilant corporate governance, including internal and external audit functions in ensuring the quality, integrity, transparency, and reliability of the financial reporting process. As an active participant in corporate governance and front-line combatants in the recent struggle against occupational fraud, corporate abuse, and FSF, forensic accountants must play an important role in improving the quality and quantity of public financial information.

Action Items

- Establishment of responsible corporate governance, vigilant board of directors and audit committee, diligent management, and adequate and effective internal and external audit functions to prevent, detect, correct, and report FSF.
- Utilization of alert, skeptical external audit function, responsible legal counsel, adequate and effective internal control structure and external regulatory procedures, and forensic accounting to combat fraud.
- Implementation of appropriate corporate strategies for correction of the committed FSF, elimination of the probability of its future occurrences, and restore confidence in the financial reporting process.

Endnotes

1. Committee of Sponsoring Organizations of the Treadway Commission (COSO). 2010. *Fraudulent Financial Reporting: 1998–2007: An Analysis of U.S. Public Companies.* www.coso.org
2. American Institute of Certified Public Accountants (AICPA). 2002. *Statement on Auditing Standards No. 99: Consideration of Fraud in a Financial Statement Audit.* Available at https://www.aicpa.org/Research/Standards/AuditAttest/DownloadableDocuments/AU-00316.pdf
3. National Commission on Fraudulent Financial Reporting. 1987. *Report of the National Commission on Fraudulent Financial Reporting.* https://www.coso.org/Publications/NCFFR.pdf
4. American institute of Certified Public Accountants (AICPA). 2017. *Consideration of Fraud in a Financial Statement Audit. AU-C Section 240.* https://www.aicpa.org/Research/Standards/AuditAttest/DownloadableDocuments/AU-C-00240.pdf
5. Z. Rezaee. 2002. *Financial Statement Fraud: Prevention and Detection* (New York, NY: John Wiley & Sons).
6. Z. Rezaee, and R. Riley. 2009. *Financial Statement Fraud: Prevention and Detection* (2nd ed., Hoboken, NJ: John Wiley & Sons, Inc.).

7. Ibid.

8. COSO. 1987. *The Report of the National Commission on Fraudulent Financial Reporting* (Washington, DC: COSO).

9. COSO. 2010. *The Report of the National Commission on Fraudulent Financial Reporting* (Washington, DC: COSO).

10. COSO. May, 2010. "Fraudulent Financial Reporting 1998-2007." https://www.coso.org/Documents/COSO-Fraud-Study-2010-001 .pdf

11. Ibid.

12. Z. Rezaee. 2002.

13. Ibid.

14. Z. Rezaee. 2002. "Internal Auditors' Roles in Prevention, Detection, and Correction of Financial Statement Fraud," *Internal Auditing* 17, no. 3, pp. 13–20.

15. Association of Certified Fraud Examiners (ACFE). 2016. *Report to the Nations on Occupational Fraud and Abuse.* http://www.acfe.com/ rttn2016.aspx, (accessed March 14, 2018).

16. Z. Rezaee. 2018. *Corporate Governance in the Aftermath of the Global Financial Crisis* (four volumes, New York, NY: Business Expert Press).

17. Z. Rezaee. 2007. *Corporate Governance Post-Sarbanes-Oxley.* Hoboken, NJ: John Wiley &Sons.

18. Rezaee and Riley. 2009.

19. Z. Rezaee, and B. Kedia. 2012. "The Role of Corporate Governance Participants in Preventing and Detecting Financial Statement Fraud." *Journal of Forensic and Investigative Accounting* 4, no. 2, pp. 176–205.

20. Ibid.

21. Ibid.

22. E. Dash. August 27, 2006. "Who Signed Off on Those Options?" *The New York Times.* Available at https://www.nytimes.com/2006/08/27/ business/yourmoney/27mercury.html

23. Ibid.

24. Ibid.

25. A.P. Lebowitz. August 3, 2005. "The WorldCom Directors Settlement: The Lead Plaintiff's Perspective," *NAPPA Report* 9.

26. Ibid.
27. Ibid.
28. Ibid.
29. Institute of Internal Auditors (IIA). 1985. *Statement of Internal Auditing Standards No. 3: Deterrence, Detection, Investigation and Reporting of Fraud* (Altamonte Springs, FL: IIA).
30. IIA. April 8, 2002. "Recommendations for Improving Corporate Governance." A Position Paper Presented by the IIA to the U.S. Congress. http://www.theiia.org/ecm/guide-pc.cfm?doc_id=3602
31. Z. Rezaee. 2002. "Internal Auditors' Roles in Prevention, Detection, and Correction of Financial Statement Fraud," *Internal Auditing* 17, no. 3, pp. 13–20.
32. American Institute of Certified Public Accountants (AICPA). 1997. *Statement on Auditing Standards No. 82: Consideration of Fraud in a Financial Statement Audit.* Available at https://www.aicpa.org/Research/Standards/AuditAttest/DownloadableDocuments/AU-C-00240.pdf
33. AICPA, 2002.
34. Ibid.
35. Public Company Accounting Oversight Board (PCAOB). 2011. *Looking Ahead: Auditor Oversight.* http://pcaobus.org/News/Speech/Pages/04042011_DotyLookingAhead.aspx
36. Ibid.
37. AICPA, 2002.
38. P.K. Jain, A. Jain, and Z. Rezaee. 2016. "Value-Relevance of Corporate Social Responsibility: Evidence from Short Selling," *Journal of Management Accounting Research* 28, no. 2, pp. 29–52.
39. ACFE. n.d. *Career Path—Forensic Accountant.* http://www.acfe.com/career-path-forensic-accountant.aspx#job, (accessed July 7, 2018).
40. Certified Fraud Examiner, Fraud Detection Services, Fraud Auditor. 2003. http://www.ltplanning.com/audit.htm, (accessed June 25, 2018).
41. Ibid.
42. ACFE. n.d. *Career Path—Public-Sector-Investigator.* http://www.acfe.com/career-path-public-sector-investigator.aspx, (accessed June 26, 2018).

43. ACFE. n.d. *Career Path—Private-Sector-Investigator*. http://www.acfe
.com/career-path-private-sector-investigator.aspx, (accessed June 26,
2018).

44. L.A. Bebchuk, and A. Ferrell. 2014. "Rethinking Basic," *The Business
Lawyer* 69, no. 3, pp. 671–97.

45. Ibid.

46. Security and Exchange Commission (SEC). 2013. *SEC Announces
Enforcement Initiatives to Combat Financial Reporting and Microcap
Fraud and Enhance Risk Analysis*. Available at https://www.sec.gov/
news/press-release/2013-2013-121htm

47. Ibid.

48. SEC. 2017. *Securities and Exchange Commission Division of
Enforcement—Enforcement Manual*. https://www.sec.gov/divisions/
enforce/enforcementmanual.pdf

49. Ibid.

50. Ibid.

51. Securities and Exchange Commission. 2017. *Enforcement Manual*.
Office of Chief Counsel. https://www.sec.gov/divisions/enforce/
enforcementmanual.pdf

CHAPTER 4

Challenges and Opportunities in Forensic Accounting

Executive Summary

High-quality financial information is the lifeblood of capital markets, and that lifeblood can be adversely affected by the existence and persistence of financial statement fraud (FSF). Forensic accounting has made impressive progress in the past two decades in the aftermath of financial scandals at the turn of the twenty-first century and the 2007 to 2009 global financial crisis. Forensic accounting has moved to the center stage of accounting as the most challenging, exciting, and rewarding field of accounting. This chapter presents emerging issues in forensic accounting in the areas of litigation consulting, expert witnessing, valuation, and fraud investigation.

Introduction

Forensic accounting has evolved in the past decade as primarily a fraud investigation to the full pledged nonfraud accounting and investigative activities. There are still many challenges in forensic accounting, and this chapter presents these challenges and the related opportunities. Challenges presented in this chapter are forensic accountants' involvement with risk assessment, cyberattacks, corporate governance, and information technology (IT). This chapter also presents emerging issues in fraud and nonfraud forensic accounting services.

Forensic Accounting Challenges and Opportunities

Forensic accounting fraud and nonfraud services are challenging and rewarding. Owing to advancements in technology, forensic accountants
need improved skills to properly and accurately use IT, Big Data, and
data analytics to improve the effectiveness of their forensic accounting
services. Analytical skills are often used to tackle Big Data, which is becoming more prevalent in businesses, particularly in larger firms. Specific
skills include database manipulation and slice and dice. These techniques
are IT-related, because the accounting field is moving toward data analytics, data mining, and manipulation of data instead of codifying data.[1]
Owing to this advancement in technology, forensic accountants' job opportunities are increasing. According to Association of Chartered Certified Accountants (ACCA), the rise of corporate governance is leading to
increasing demand. Corporate governance measures are designed to hold
corporate gatekeepers accountable and to oust unethical and illegal business practices. Forensic accountants investigate these practices and aid in
the trail process during litigation procedures.[2]

The rise of emphasis on corporate governance is a direct result of recent well-known fraud cases such as Enron and WorldCom, among others. Fraud cases presented in previous chapters suggest that ineffective
corporate governance has contributed to the existence and persistence of
financial statement fraud (FSF). Forensic accountants understand that
fraud happens from an ineffective corporate governance, insufficient internal controls, and improper regulations and standards. Forensic accountants often advocate for open communication, established oversight, and
a set of rules that punish the guilty to solidify corporate governance. If
fraud happens, often because of failures in corporate governance, forensic
accountants will review financial statements, identify red flags and areas of
high risk for fraud potential, and follow red flags to fraudulent behavior.[3]

Forensic Accounting Opportunities

Forensic accountants have provided a variety of fraud and nonfraud services, including FSF investigation, litigation consulting, expert witnessing, and valuation, among other services. These services have contributed
to the success of businesses and individuals as well as the accounting

profession. Many professional organizations, particularly the Big 4, have established expertise and market niche in forensic accounting. Deloitte has a project deliver analyst position, which requires assistance with federal investigations, anti-money laundering (AML) compliance, support tasks, and analysis of fraud, whereas KPMG, PwC, and EY have similar positions.[4] In the government sector, the Tennessee Bureau of Investigation (TBI) has forensic services divisions located in Nashville, Knoxville, and Memphis, in which employees investigate crime scenes, respond to violent crime, and examine medical material.[5] The Committee of Sponsoring Organizations of the Treadway Commission (COSO) released its "Fraud Risk Management Guide" in September 2016, that encourages engagement of all corporate gatekeepers including the board of directors, management and internal and external auditors, legal counsel, and forensic accountants in FSF risk assessment and management.[6]

The Securities and Exchange Commission (SEC) has recently taken three initiatives, namely, the Financial Reporting and Audit Task Force, the Microcap Fraud Task Force, and the Centre for Risk and Quantitative Analytics to investigate and combat FSF.[7] Forensic accounting practices are exciting and rewarding. The forensic accounting field is experiencing rapid growth. The rise of technology has increased the number of jobs and requirements for forensic accountants. The ACFE released a global study in 2017 that showed a 31-percent increase in compensation when a forensic accountant obtains a Certified Fraud Examiner (CFE) certification.[8] The average annual salary for a forensic accountant, according to Glassdoor statistics, is $80,464.[9]

Challenges for Forensic Accountants

Forensic accountants are facing many challenges in successfully performing their professional services. The most prevailing challenges for forensic accountants are in the areas of fraud investigation, risk assessment, and corporate governance, among others, addressed in this section.

Financial Fraud Investigation

FSF is defined in previous chapter as deliberate misstatement or omission of amounts or disclosures of financial statements to deceive financial statement users, particularly investors and creditors. There is a variety of

FSF schemes as discussed in the previous chapters. The motivation to commit FSF not only comes from pressures that are placed on management to succeed but also comes from departmental budget requirements including income and profit goals. FSF is harmful in many ways; for example it[10]:

1. Undermines the reliability, quality, transparency, and integrity of the financial reporting process. An increasing number of financial restatements and recent enforcement acts by the SEC against big corporations (e.g., Enron, WorldCom, Xerox, ImClone, Global Crossing, Qwest, Halliburton, Bristol-Myers, Tyco, Dynegy, Adelphia Communications, and Computer Associates) for alleged FSF has severely undermined the public confidence in the veracity of financial reports.

2. Jeopardizes the integrity and objectivity of the auditing profession, especially auditors and auditing firms. Andersen, one of the Big-5 CPA firms, during the past several months, has dismantled its international network and allowed offices to join rival firms. The jury's guilty verdict of obstruction of justice effectively ended Andersen's audit practice.

3. Diminishes the confidence of the capital markets, as well as market participants, in the reliability of financial information. The capital market and market participants, including investors, creditors, employees, and pensioners, are affected by the quality and transparency of financial information they use in making investment decisions.

4. Makes the capital market less efficient. Auditors reduce the information risk that may be associated with the published financial statements and thus make them more transparent. The information risk is the likelihood that financial statements are inaccurate, false, misleading, biased, and deceptive. By applying the same financial standards to diverse businesses and by reducing the information risk, accountants contribute to the efficiency of our capital markets.

5. Adversely affects the nation's economic growth and prosperity. Accountants are expected to make financial statements among corporations more comparable by applying the same set of accounting standards to diverse businesses. This enhanced comparability makes

business more transparent, the capital markets more efficient, free enterprise system possible, and the economy more vibrant and prosperous. The efficiency of our capital markets depends on receiving objective, reliable, and transparent financial information. Thus, the accounting profession, especially practicing auditors, plays an important role in our free enterprise system and capital markets. However, Enron, WorldCom, and Global Crossing debacles cast some doubt that the role of accountants can be compromised.

6. Results in huge litigation costs. Corporations and their auditors are being sued for alleged FSF and related audit failures by a diverse group of litigants, including class action suits by small investors and suits by the U.S. Department of Justice. Investors are also given the right to sue and recover damages from those who aided and abetted securities fraud.

7. Destroys careers of individuals involved in FSF such as top executives being barred from serving on the board of directors of any public companies or auditors being barred from practice of public accounting. Several senior executives of Adelphia Communications were arrested on July 24, 2002, for allegedly committing fraud by stealing hundreds of millions of dollars from the battered cable company and engaging in financial shenanigans.

8. Causes bankruptcy or loss of substantial economic losses by the company engaged in FSF. WorldCom, with $107 billion in assets and $41 billion in debt, finally filed for Chapter 11 bankruptcy protection on July 21, 2002. WorldCom's bankruptcy is the largest U.S. bankruptcy ever, almost twice the size of Enron.

9. Encourages regulatory intervention. Regulatory agencies (e.g., the SEC) considerably influence the financial reporting process and related audit functions. The current perceived crisis in the financial reporting process and audit functions has encouraged lawmakers to establish accounting reform legislation (Sarbanes–Oxley [SOX] Act of 2002). The SOX Act will drastically change the self-regulating environment of the accounting profession to a regulatory framework under the SEC oversight function.

10. Causes destructions in the normal operations and performance of alleged companies. Alleged FSF of Enron, WorldCom, Global

Crossing, and Adelphia has caused these high-profile companies to file bankruptcy, and their top executives have been fined and, in some cases, indicted for violation of Securities Acts.

11. Raises serious doubt about the efficacy of financial statement audits. The financial community is demanding that high-quality audits and auditors should improve their audit effectiveness and efficacy to produce the needed assurance.

12. Erodes public confidence and trust in the accounting and auditing profession. One message that comes through loud and clear these days in response to the increasing number of financial restatements and alleged FSF is that the public confidence in the financial reporting process and related audit functions is substantially eroded.

The COSO released its "Fraud Risk Management Guide" in September 2016, which suggests a comprehensive monitoring and assessment approach in managing fraud risk, including FSF by all corporate gatekeepers from the board of directors to management, internal auditors, external auditors, and others such as short sellers and forensic accountants.[11] All corporate gatekeepers play an important role in preventing, detecting, and correcting FSF, as depicted in Exhibit 4.1.

FSF is intentional wrongful acts by management to mislead shareholders and other stakeholders by presenting materially misstated financial reports. This type of fraud is intentionally committed to benefit the company to the detrimental of shareholders or engaging in fraud against the company involving misappropriation of assets. The elements of fraud are as follows:

- A false representation of a material nature
- Knowledge that the representation is false or reckless disregard for the truth (Scienter)
- Reliance on the false representation by the victim
- Financial damages are incurred (to the benefit of the perpetrator).
- The act was intentional.

The important element of management and occupational fraud is the intent and knowingly engaging in fraud. Although "intent" is an element

Exhibit 4.1

Financial Statement Fraud: Functions, Actions, and Consequences

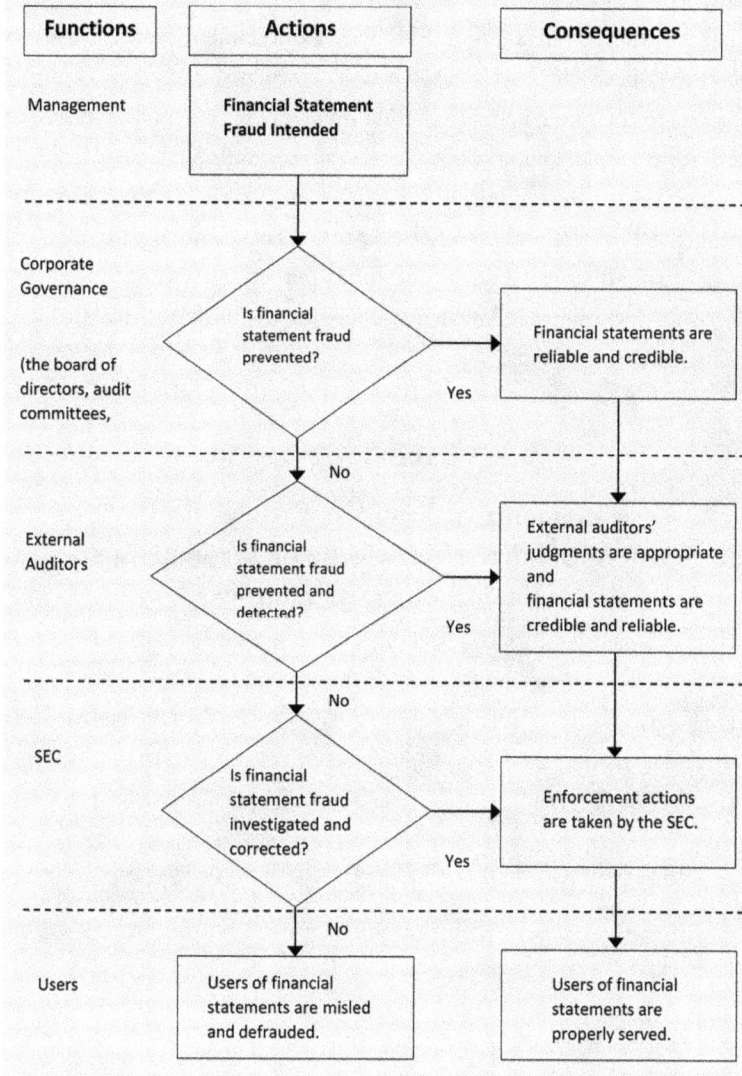

Functions	Actions	Consequences

Management — **Financial Statement Fraud Intended**

Corporate Governance

(the board of directors, audit committees,

Is financial statement fraud prevented? — Yes → Financial statements are reliable and credible.

No

External Auditors — Is financial statement fraud prevented and detected? — Yes → External auditors' judgments are appropriate and financial statements are credible and reliable.

No

SEC — Is financial statement fraud investigated and corrected? — Yes → Enforcement actions are taken by the SEC.

No

Users — Users of financial statements are misled and defrauded. — Users of financial statements are properly served.

of fraud, the presence of "intent" is difficult to prove in fraud cases by "direct" evidence. Thus, forensic accountants usually focus on other three elements of fraud, as depicted in Exhibit 4.2. The three elements are "The Act," "The Conversion," and "The Concealment" that are the metrics used by forensic accountants in analyzing corporate fraud. The "Act" is usually the theft or engaging in FSF. The "Concealment" usually involves efforts to conceal the "Act." "Conversion" is when the fraudsters convert the assets to their own benefit. The Act involves the actual perpetration of fraud, for example, taking cash or the misappropriation of assets. Conversion involves converting business resources for personal use and/or transferring the business and its resources to others. Concealment involves the actions and steps taken by the fraud perpetrators to hide fraud by destroying documents and evidence, changing the business structure, and altering financial records.

Exhibit 4.2

Elements of Fraud as Proxies for Intent/Scienter/Knowledge of Wrongdoing (Dimond of Fraud Actions)

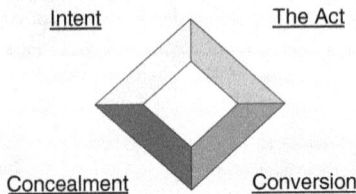

Intent   The Act

Concealment   Conversion

Source: This Dimond of fraud actions is developed based on the original triangle of characteristics of the crime by Albrecht, S., C.O Albrecht. C. C.C Albrecht. 2006. Fraud Examination, 2nd Edition, Thompson, South Wetern, Canada.

Digital Forensics

Digital forensic is the merging area of practice for forensic accountants that create both challenges and opportunities for them. Particularly, digital analysis can serve as an effective tool in identifying material errors and irregularities and detecting fraud. Digital forensics, including computer forensics and network forensics, is a digital data analytics technique used in investigating and analyzing evidence in online computer networks. There are multiple types of software that can be used to analyze digital data. An example includes the Forensic Toolkit, which often is called the FTK. The FTK is produced by ACCESSDATA, which is a forensic service firm founded in 1987 to help clients address fraud using its software. The toolkit itself has been ported over to mobile and e-technology platforms to further its mobility. According to Grant Thornton, a modestly sized accounting firm, the use of FTK is prevalent in its offices.[12] In terms of software function, it locates evidence and then analyzes the location it originated from. The evidence is stored in a central database making it easy to access. Along with ease of accessing, having a central database reduces cost of maintenance. For more information pertaining to the forensic toolkits functionality and Grant Thornton's opinion on the software, please visit accessdata.com.[13]

Benford's law, one of the most commonly used techniques, is used in digital analysis. In applying the Benford's law, a forensic accountant could extract the first number from a dataset using the "Left" function in excel, and then execute a "Sumif" function to calculate the percentage of numbers that begin with 1–9. In a normal dataset, there will be more 1's than 2's, 2's than 3's, 3's than 4's, consecutively. Other digital analysis techniques include:

> Searching for duplicate transactions, searching for rounded amounts, and performing ratio analysis in which the ratio of the highest value to the lowest (maximum/minimum), the ratio of the highest value to the next highest (maximum/second highest), and the ratio of the current year to the previous year are analyzed.[14]

The importance of digital forensics is ever increasing in the current business environment, because companies are moving toward a reduced, or paperless environment. A byproduct of this shift is an increasing proportion of digital to nondigital evidence. A fraud examiner proficient in digital forensics can recover seemingly deleted documents, e-mails, files, programs, and so on, by having proficient knowledge of a computer's registry. This change in environment works in the favor of the fraud examiner because, previously, if a paper file and its backups were destroyed the file would be gone. However, in computerized systems it is much more difficult to delete all traces and backups of a file owing to the sheer amount of storage possibilities.[15] Digital fraud is growing as e-commerce strategies are becoming more common business practices, and thus digital fraud perpetrators are fined for engaging in digital fraud transmitting by means of wire, radio, or television communication in interstate or foreign commerce, any writings, signs, signals, pictures, or sounds for the purpose of executing such scheme or artifice.[16]

Big Data and Data Analytics

IT advances (e.g., cloud, social media, and analytics) enable organizations to have an unprecedented amount of structured, semi-structured, and unstructured data. The emergence of "high-volume, high-velocity, and high-variety" information that can be processed electronically to facilitate decision making is usually described as Big Data.[17] Big Data has also received common acceptance and practical application in the business community. For example, more than 98 percent of all stored information is electronic, compared with about 25 percent of such information, which was digital in 2000.[18] Because traditional rules-based relational database techniques, such as matching, sorting, filtering, and query design, often result in false positives or missed fraud detection opportunities, forensic accountants nowadays incorporate data visualization, predictive analytics, behavior analytics, content analytics, social network analysis, geo-spatial analytics, and numerous advanced antifraud techniques.[19]

Forensic accountants are now able to obtain a huge amount of both structured (e.g., general ledger or transaction data) and unstructured data (e.g., e-mail, voice, or free-text fields in a database), together with an increasing amount of nontraditional data sources such as third-party watch lists, news media, free-text payment descriptions, e-mail communications, and social media. As a result, forensic accountants use advanced technological tools in the investigation. For example, forensic accountants use social media and web monitoring, voice searching and analysis, visualization, and reporting tools.[20] There is a shortage of forensic accountants who possess Big Data/analytical skills and are able to use sophisticated analytical tools to effectively and accurately identify potential risks and proactively search for irregularities and assess and manage their risk profile. The growing demand and inadequate supply of Big Data professionals raises the question whether there is adequate training related to Big Data at the undergraduate/graduate level in the forensic accounting education. The integration of Big Data into the forensic accounting and business curriculum supports the market demand in these two areas and keeps the business curriculum aligned with the practices.

The following examples illustrate the use of Big Data (analytics) in the forensic accounting practice. First, when forensic accountants investigate fraud, corruption, or bribery cases, they take industry-specific norms or regulations into consideration and use keyword phrases to identify potential frauds. Second, by utilizing historical activities or transaction data, forensic accountants can use predictive modeling and other advanced analytics to detect suspicious and anomalous transactions, high-risk events, or potential fraudulent behaviors or activities. Third, by mining across multiple sources of databases (e.g., customer or third-party databases), forensic accountants can use entity resolution algorithms to identify hidden relationships, addresses, and aliases and investigate conflicts of interest, fake identities, or sanctioned individuals/entities.

Fourth, forensic accountants use social network analytics to detect hidden relationships, bogus vendors, or fake bank accounts when they analyze both structured and unstructured data in the format of visuals and links from social media. Fifth, a large amount of unstructured text data is available from the free-text field of journal entries, payment description, expense details, e-mails, social media, documents, presentations, and hard drives of individual employees or the organizations. Forensic accountants use text mining or text analytics with heuristic rules and statistical techniques to discover the sentiments and conceptual meanings of large amounts of text data, which help to identify potential frauds or noncompliance in the organization. Finally, besides traditional simple spreadsheets or static charts and graphs, forensic accountants use data visualization techniques and interactive dashboards to present evidence in an easy-to-understand manner.

Data analytics has the potential to significantly improve the effectiveness and efficiency services performed by forensic accountants. Data analytics have been used by accountants and auditors for many years, and forensic accountants should use more advanced data analytics in identifying red flags, patterns of errors, irregularities, and fraud. Data warehousing and data mining techniques are the process of identifying and analyzing patterns in massive datasets to predict future norms. Data mining is the process of exploring large datasets to discover patterns and predictive analytics through use of algorithms. This process has been exaggerated through the many prevalent software.[21] The most popular software includes Microsoft SharePoint, Dundas BI, and IBM Cognos Analytics. Data warehousing is a database linking relationships to queries. Data warehouses are not used to process transactions, and it uses historical transaction data to consolidate useable data to be analyzed.[22]

Forensic accountants use the above-mentioned techniques during investigations. For data mining, Dundas BI can be used to analyze data. This software can provide real-time data analysis and can use visualizations to aid in easy understanding of complex data. According to the Dundas website, dashboards can be combined with data and exported into different business applications.[23] The applications include Microsoft SharePoint and HTML5. Microsoft SharePoint is used to create websites for businesses.[24] The website can use HTML5, which is the latest evolution of HTML and is a markup language that allows the usage of documentation.[25] Forensic accountants can use these powerful tools during investigations to articulate important data through visualizations that are easy to understand.

The use of analytical procedures as substantive evidence gathering requires that forensic accountants pay attention to underlying relationships and develop a precise and independent expectation of the account balance and related risks (i.e., the inherent and control risk). If there are any unexpected differences, they should be assessed and their impacts be evaluated. Analytical procedures provide indirect evidence and as such draw auditor attentions to things out of norm, irregularities, and red flag symptoms. In the case that an explanation for the abnormalities cannot be obtained, forensic accountants should perform other procedures to gather sufficient evidence that the abnormalities were not caused by a misstatement. Analytical procedures can be particularly effective for assertions in which potential misstatements are not apparent or where evidence is not available. When higher levels of assurance are required, analytical procedures should be applied to more predictable relationships. Relationships involving transactions subject to management discretion and those pertaining to balance sheet are less predictable by nature.[26]

Scholars have used a wide range of data sources, well-developed core analytics capabilities, and integration of the Internet of things (IoT) and artificial intelligence (AI) into processes to improve their engagement and interactions with customers.[27] The following are the advantages of using data analytics:[28]

1. Competitive advantage from analytics continues to grow as more than half (59 percent) of executive report their company is using analytics to gain a competitive advantage.
2. Analytics is driving customer engagement because the most analytically mature organizations are twice as likely to report strong customer engagement as the least analytically mature organizations.
3. Analytically mature organizations use more data sources to engage customers.
4. Sharing data can improve influence with customers and other groups.

EY conducted a Global Forensic Data Analytics Survey in 2018.[29] The survey focused on technological advancement and its effect on businesses. As technology advances, the risk profile of business changes. The most important risks affecting firms today are data privacy and cybersecurity, at a 40 percent increase and 38 percent, respectively. However, the effectiveness of forensic data analytics on fraud risk management reveals that for the largest category, internal investigations has 50 percent of respondents claiming that the FDA method is somewhat effective. This is indicative of a lack of connection between fraud risk profile, fraud risk management of the profile, and the use of forensic data analytics to mitigate the inherent risks of technology.[30] In practice, it is important for forensic accountants to use the necessary skills to work in the era of technological era.

Corporate Governance Challenges

Corporate governance has evolved as a central theme for public companies in the aftermath of the 2007 to 2009 global financial crisis. In today's global environment, business organizations are under scrutiny and profound pressures from lawmakers, regulators, the investment community, and their diverse stakeholders to accept accountability and responsibility for their corporate governance effectiveness and financial reporting process. Corporate governance is a process (journey) of managing corporate affairs to create shareholder value while protecting interests of other stakeholders. Corporate governance can strengthen the safety, efficiency, depth, and liquidity of capital markets and reliability of public financial information. Effective corporate governance ensures strong investor protection, giving rise to high-quality financial reports, which enables investors to make sound investment decisions. Forensic accountants can investigate corporate irregularities, illegal acts, and fraud as well as prevent, discover, and correct them to improve the reliability of financial reports used by investors.

Sound investment decisions by investors improve efficiency of capital markets that results in economic prosperity and growth for the nation. Corporate governance has been transformed from simply a routine set of compliance requirements to a strategic business imperative. The integrity, reliability, and transparency of financial reports is a function of corporate governance effectiveness. Corporate governance measures and practices have become a mandate for both public and private firms, regardless of their size, type, or location. No longer is corporate governance just seen as one of many compliance requirements. Today, good corporate governance measures and procedures are being actively integrated into the corporate culture, business model, and the environment of companies across the country and around the world to ensure accountability and sustainability. Corporate gatekeepers are the focal point of these efforts and the conduits of company information to shareholders, management, customers, suppliers, financiers, government, and the community.

Competition among global capital markets can be healthy in producing an adequate level of protection for investors through the right balance of corporate governance and regulatory reforms. Corporate governance functions constitute an important element of the corporate governance structure. There are seven essential corporate governance functions: oversight, managerial, compliance, internal audit, advisory, external audit, and monitoring. A well-balanced implementation of these seven interrelated functions produces effective corporate governance, reliable financial reports, and credible audit services. This integrated approach underscores and reaffirms the primary goal of corporations to create sustainable shareholder value while protecting the interests of other stakeholders. Given that the primary purpose of any business, particularly public companies, is to create substantial and enduring value, the goal of corporate governance is to ensure that all participants are working to achieve this goal.

The seven interactive functions should be properly integrated into the overall corporate culture, business environment, and corporate strategy and accountability. Three of these seven functions, however, are essential to the achievement of sustainable and long-term corporate performance. These corporate governance functions are the oversight function assumed by the board of directors, the managerial function delegated to management, and the monitoring function exercised by shareholders. Effective corporate governance should develop a right balance between the achievement of short-term targets and long-term sustainable performance. To effectively fulfill their fiduciary duties, corporate governance participants should lead from the front and by example in managing the organization for the best interests of its stakeholders. Corporate governance should create an appropriate balance of power-sharing that:

- provides shareholder democracy in freely electing directors (e.g., the majority voting system).
- enables the board of directors to make strategic decisions and oversee and consult with management without micromanaging.
- empowers management to run the company.

The participants in the corporate governance process are the board of directors, executives, stakeholders/shareholders, and gatekeepers, including internal auditors, external auditors, financial analysts, legal counsel, financial advisors, and regulators. Forensic accountants can provide consulting services to all corporate governance participants from the board of directors to management and internal and external auditor and legal counsel in effectively discharging their fiduciary duties. Forensic accountants in investigating corporate misconduct, irregularities, fraud, and illegal acts can improve the effectiveness of corporate governance. Forensic accountants can provide a wide range of services to corporate governance participants, including anticorruption compliance, forensic technology investigation, fraud prevention, and dispute services. Compliance services aid in the minimization of risk associated with manipulation of laws, regulations, and corporate governance. Fraud perpetrators often commit fraud on the occupation and management level, so strict compliance is necessary for those positions. Compliance minimizes risks by testing internal control, enhancing policies regarding corporate governance and fraud risk management, and correcting fraud loopholes. Compliance services are usually linked with investigations. Investigations can vary in subject, but usually revolve around management and employees.[31]

Whistleblowing Program, Policies and Procedures

Much of fraud is being discovered through unanimous tips from employees, customers, suppliers, and others. The audit committee of public companies is responsible for overseeing the establishment and enforcement of whistle-blower programs in compliance with the requirements of SOX and SEC-related rules.[32] SOX created the opportunity for confidential and anonymous submissions of complaints by requiring that the company's audit committee establish procedures for receiving, recording, retaining, and treating such complaints. Section 301 of SOX requires audit committees of public companies to establish effective programs and procedures for handling the concerns and complaints of whistle-blowers.[33] Pursuant to the passage of SOX, concerned employees are enabled to report financial and accounting irregularities as well as fraud without undue fear of suffering demotion, suspension, harassment, threats, loss of job, or any other form of retribution.

To implement provisions of SOX pertaining to whistle-blowers effectively, public companies should establish whistle-blower programs and procedures that enable employees to report suspected incidents of misconduct anonymously. These programs and procedures encompass establishing an effective hotline with a toll-free number and the capability to accept collect calls, a fax number, a regular mail address or post office box, and a confidential website. Anonymous reporting channels may be particularly useful in encouraging the reporting of wrongdoing by organizational members because anonymity should minimize personal "costs" of reporting, such as retaliation and other potential penalties. A benefit of such channels is that employees often discover FSF before other monitors (e.g., internal auditors, external auditors, and/or regulators) and, consequently, often can inform the organization earlier than others.

The past decade, particularly the post-SOX period, provides a better understanding of what whistle-blowers are and the important role they can play in preventing, reporting, and correcting corporate corruption, fraud, and financial malfeasance. Whistleblowers at Enron (Sherron Watkins) and WorldCom (Cynthia Cooper) prove that they are often the brightest, best qualified, most courageous, and most committed employees in organizations who risk their employment and life for speaking out about wrongdoings. Sections 301 and 806 of SOX and SEC-related rules require (1) the audit committee to establish procedures for the receipt, retention, and treatment of complaints received by the company relevant to accounting, internal accounting control, or auditing matters as well as confidential and anonymous submission by employees of concerns regarding questionable accounting or auditing matters; and (2) that the company provide whistle-blower protections for its employees who willingly report evidence of fraud or violations of securities laws.[34] SOX and the SEC do not require any specific procedures for whistle-blower programs and procedures and give flexibility to the listed companies and their audit committees to establish whistle-blower programs and procedures that are suitable for and tailored to their particular situations.[35]

The SOX of 2002 and SEC-related rules require that the audit committee establish and maintain appropriate whistle-blower programs for the receipt, process, and retention of complaints regarding internal control accounting and auditing matters.[36] Such programs must establish procedures and mechanisms that encompass the confidential and anonymous submission of concerns on questionable accounting and auditing matters by employees. The SEC requires that the audit committee establish specific mechanisms tailored and suitable to the company's circumstances and needs for whistle-blower programs. The whistle-blowing program must be established in compliance with both the SOX of 2002 and the Dodd–Frank (DOF) Act of 2010. Section 301 of the SOX contain whistle-blowing provisions that require the audit committee to establish policies and procedures regarding the receipt, retention, and treatment of complaints about violations of accounting and auditing standards, and Section 806 prohibits retaliations against whistle-blowers.[37]

Section 806 of the DOF of 2010 provides protections for whistleblowers in securities fraud cases and has directed the SEC to establish rules regarding confidential and anonymous submissions of violations of security laws and conduct of fraudulent and unethical activities by public companies.[38] Whistleblowers are protected and rewarded for informing the SEC of corporate wrongdoings. Forensic accountants can assist the audit committee to assess the effectiveness of the whistle-blowing policies, procedures and practices. Forensic accountants can also be source of information for the SEC in investigating and enforcing its whistle-blowing processes.

Sustainability Reporting and Assurance and Forensic Accountants

Business sustainability has garnered considerable attention in the wake of the recent global financial crisis and is now emerging as a central issue for regulators and public companies. In particular, business sustainability focuses on protecting interests of all stakeholders from shareholders to creditors, employees, customers, suppliers, government, environment and society. Thus, effective sustainability performance is expected to better align interests of management with those of all stakeholders and better protect them from receiving fraudulent financial information. Thus, effective sustainability performance improves sustainable financial health, corporate governance, quality of financial information, enhances the integrity and efficiency of the capital market, and improves investor confidence. Poor sustainability performance adversely affects corporate governance, the company's potential, performance, financial reports and accountability and can pave the way for business failure, fraudulent public financial information, inefficiency in capital markets and loss of investor confidence. The important question address in section is "Do firms that issue sustainability report engage less in FSF and what forensic accountants can do to prevent and detect FSF in the context of sustainability reporting and assurance?"

The holistic and comprehensive definition of sustainability reporting is the process of disclosing information relevant to both financial and nonfinancial key performance indicators (KPIs) for all five areas of multiple bottom line performance: economic, governance, social, ethics, and environmental (EGSEE).[39] Sustainability disclosures affect financial reporting quality in several ways. First, sustainability reporting reduces incentives for focus on short-term performance of manipulating earnings to meet analysts' earnings forecast. Second, sustainability reporting focuses on improving corporate governance which will reduce opportunities to engage in fraudulent financial activities. Third, sustainability disclosures reduce information asymmetry which improves quality of financial reports. Forensic accountants are capable of assisting business organizations in avoiding short-termism phenomenon, combatting fraudulent activities and minimizing information asymmetry.

The number of public companies worldwide that disclose sustainability performance information has increased significantly to more than 15,000, and today, most European companies are now disclosing their sustainability performance information. The reliability and credibility of these integrated sustainability reports need to be assured by assurance providers and forensic accountants can provide assurance on the integrated sustainability reports. To integrate sustainability into corporate culture, strategic planning and business environment forensic accountants can assist management in establishing and implementing anti-fraud policies and procedures consisting of:

- Defining sustainability shared value creation in the organization
- Identifying and assessing the positive and negative impact of trends shaping the organization's five EGSEE.
- Identifying non-financial metrics on non-financial dimensions of sustainability performance (governance, social, ethical, and environmental)
- Linking non-financial sustainability performance metrics to the sustainable financial success of the business.
- Preparing integrated sustainability reports reflecting both financial and non-financial information.
- Obtaining assurance on sustainability reports from external assurance providers including forensic accountants.

Forensic Accountants and Internal Control Reporting

Traditionally, organizations have reported their performance on economic affairs and their only focus on financial results has become complicated, irrelevant, and less value-relevant to all stakeholders including shareholders. Firm performance is measured not only by financial income, but also by the mechanisms in which business success and sustainability is measured in terms of non-financial sustainability key performance indicators pertaining to environmental, social, governance, and ethical activities. Public companies play an important role in disseminating useful, reliable, relevant, and transparent financial/quantitative and nonfinancial/qualitative information to the financial markets. Public companies are now not only report their financial statements but also the process of preparing financial statements in the context of reporting their internal control over financial reporting (ICFR).

The reliability of financial statements, the effectiveness of ICFR, and the efficacy of audits of both financial statements and ICFR under integrated financial and internal control reporting (IFICR) are vital if public companies are to attract investors and build confidence in the capital markets. Many provisions of the Sarbanes–Oxley Act of 2002 (SOX) pertain to financial reporting, including Sections 302 and 404, which require public companies' management (CEO, CFO) to certify financial statements and report on the effectiveness of the company's ICFR and require auditors to attest to and report on both financial statements and ICFR. Section 302 requires that the audit committee oversees the work of management and the independent auditor as related to ICFR. The audit committee's oversight of Section 404 is essential, as mandatory ICFR is becoming an integral part of financial reporting. The effectiveness of the IFICR depends on the vigilant oversight function of the board of directors, particularly the audit committee, the responsible and accountable managerial function of senior executives, the credible external audit function of the independent auditor, and the objective internal audit function of internal auditors.

IFICR reports are expected to reduce the information risk that financial information is misleading, biased, incomplete, inaccurate, or fraudulent. In this context, audits reduce financial information asymmetries between management and shareholders and thus help investors to make more informed decisions that in turn make the capital markets more efficient and add to the nation's economic prosperity. Management is ultimately and directly responsible for the reliability and quality of all internal and external financial reports including IFICR. Internal auditors assist management in the proper assessment, documentation and reporting of IFICR. External auditors lend more credibility to IFICR by providing reasonable assurance on the effectiveness of internal controls and the reliability of financial statements. Companies of all sizes and types worldwide benefit from an effective IFICR. Proper preparation and reporting of IFICR requires public companies to obtain:

- Management certification of financial statements in certifying reliability, completeness, and accuracy of financial statements.
- Management certification of the effectiveness of internal control over financial reporting.
- Audit report providing reasonable assurance that financial statements are free from material misstatement whether caused by error or fraud and an opinion that financial statements are prepared in conformity with applicable accounting standards.
- Audit report on the effectiveness of internal control over financial reporting.
- Audit committee review and approval of both management and auditor reports on financial statements and internal control over financial reporting.
- The board of directors' declaration that management and auditor reports on financial statements and internal control over financial reporting be filed with regulators and disseminated to shareholders.

Forensic accountant can adopt new approaches to assessing risks and controls. Forensic accountants can monitor how technological innovation is changing businesses and their corresponding changes to risks and controls. Forensic accountants can deliver new value by implementing and creating digital tools for internal control risk assessment and management. Changes in the risk environment, technological advancements and increasing regulatory pressure have created new opportunities for forensic accountants to develop new capabilities in internal control reporting.

Forensic Accountants and Antifraud Program and Plan

The persistence of this fraud is still a significant concern for the business community and the accounting profession and has eroded investor confidence in corporate reports. From Enron and WorldCom in 2001, to Madoff and Satyam in 2009, Olympus in 2011 and Volkswagen in 2015, over the past decade, financial reporting fraud has been a dominant news item. There has been ample evidence that financial reporting fraud has undermined the integrity and quality of financial reports and has contributed to substantial economic losses. Since the passage of the SOX Act, which was primarily intended to combat financial reporting fraud, there are more incidents of FRF. Companies of all types and sizes are susceptible to employee fraud including embezzlements, thefts, and misappropriations of assets as well as Financial Reporting Fraud (FRF), or "cooking the books," to show a rosy picture of the company so that it appears more attractive to investors than it really is.

Financial reporting fraud can occur in situations where there are unexplained accounting anomalies, unusually rapid revenue or profit growth, weak internal controls, and aggressive financial actions by senior management, among other things. The very viability of the business as well as the safety of financial markets in general are threatened when the existence and persistence of FRF go undetected. Financial reporting fraud can be detected with effective corporate governance, which includes effective antifraud policies and programs by the board of directors, management, and auditors. Effective antifraud programs, focusing on fraud awareness and education in the workplace environment, whistle-blowing policies and procedures of encouraging employees to report suspicious behavior without fear of reprisals, adequate internal control procedures designed to prevent and detect fraud, and conducting surprise audits are all examples of actions that the board of directors, management, and other corporate gatekeepers can take to significantly reduce FRF. Forensic accountant can assist public companies to prevent and detect FRF and to minimize its detrimental effects by:

- Assessing existing antifraud programs and controls, establish effective fraud prevention and detection policies and procedures, and communicate with the audit committee and independent auditors.

- Conducting a fraud risk assessment process to identify the company's risks and establish related control activities to effectively prevent and detect fraud.
- Evaluating and testing the design and operating effectiveness of internal controls to prevent and detect fraud.
- Standardizing the processes for fraud incident investigation and remediation and enable prompt responses to allegations or suspicions of fraud.
- Establishing antifraud programs and controls relevant to both financial reporting fraud and occupational fraud.
- Establishing antifraud deterrence; prevention, detection, and correction mechanisms driven from the corporate culture of setting an appropriate tone at the top; promoting competent and ethical behavior and reinforcing antifraud conduct; and demanding to do the right thing always.

Forensic Accountants and Enterprise Risk Management

Enterprise risk management (ERM) has recently received considerable attention from public companies, the business community, and the accounting profession. Financial scandals of the early 2000s and recent world events, including the September 11, 2001 terrorist attacks and recent cyberattacks, have generated more interest in the issue of overall ERM. Natural disasters, such as hurricanes, earthquakes, and floods, require companies to design adequate and effective disaster recovery plans and assess their risk of occurrence and their consequence on operations. Companies should conduct risk assessment periodically to identify potential risks and design appropriate controls to mitigate their adversarial impacts. The board of directors, particularly the audit committee, should oversee the company's ERM, and both internal and external auditors should be involved in assessing risks of natural disasters and the protection of important electronics and other information.

The board of directors should oversee the company's risk appetite and access timely information on current and emerging material risk exposures and risk response strategies, and should implement effective risk management processes. Forensic accountants can assist public companies and their boards of directors to effectively fulfill their oversight of risk assessment and management as stated below:

- Establishing a risk compliance board committee by delegating all responsibilities to such board committee.
- Making the entire board of directors responsible for risk oversight;
- Combination of the first two alternatives by making the whole Board responsible along with delegation of specific roles and responsibilities to Board committees.

COSO releases frequent reports regarding the effectiveness of the ERM framework on financial statements. In May 2010, the official COSO report was released, which provided details about key fraudulent events. The study found that most companies that committed fraud had assets around $100 million and of which executive management was involved in approximately 90 percent of cases (347 cases total). Of these cases, the most common fraud schemes were recognizing revenue at the improper time and manipulation of assets and expenses.[40] Forensic accountants can assist in design and implementation of the ERM that detects and prevents FSF.

Forensic Accountants and XBRL-Generated Financial Reports

Extensible business reporting language (XBRL) is an application of extensible markup language (XML) in business and financial reporting. XBRL is now commonly accepted as the electronic method of business and financial reporting worldwide. XBRL tools, techniques, and taxonomies have been developed by the XBRL International Steering Committee available at the XBRL website (www.xbrl.org). XBRL enables computer systems to assemble data electronically in instance documents, retrieve data directly from XBRL instance documents, and convert data into human-readable financial reports. In 2004, the SEC established a voluntary XBRL filing program under its Electronic Data Gathering, Analysis, and Retrieval (EDGAR) system. The Federal Deposit Insurance Corporation (FDIC) has implemented an XBRL filing system for all its banks, and European financial institutions are using XBRL in more than 25 countries.

In the United States, both regulators (SEC) and standard setters (FASB, PCAOB) have taken initiatives to address online real-time financial reporting using the XBRL format and electronic or continuous auditing. Recently, the SEC has promoted XBRL voluntary reporting and provided a faster review for companies using XBRL. It is expected that XBRL taxonomies for different industries will be further developed, and the use of the XBRL format will gain more momentum. A move toward the global acceptance of XBRL for electronic business and financial reporting requires auditors to provide assurance by conducting an integrated audit on XBRL-generated financial statements. An important issue for regulators (SEC), standard setters (FASB, PCAOB), public companies, and the accounting profession is to decide whether to require public reporting on XBRL-generated financial statements and internal control reports at a point in time (periodic filing report dates, quarterly Form 10-Q, or annual Form 10-K) or on a real-time basis. Companies, however, should use XBRL-generated financial statements and related internal controls on a real-time basis for internal purposes.

Forensic accountant can assist in an integrated audit of periodic XBRL-generated financial statements and internal controls, which requires investigation of the following:

- Internal controls over XBRL taxonomy, the tagging of data, preparation of the instance documents, the integrity of the tagged data, and the consistent application of both taxonomy and the tagged data.
- The effectiveness of both the design and operation of XBRL internal controls, including authorization procedures and selection of the appropriate taxonomy and tagged data in producing financial statements.
- The XBRL instance documents to ensure the integrity and reliability of XBRL-generated financial statements and comparability of data contained in the instance documents and the audited financial statements.
- XBRL-generated financial statements in conformity with the selected XBRL taxonomy.

Conclusion

Forensic accounting has advanced as one of the most demanding and rewarding areas of accounting practices, including fraud examination, anticorruption and antibribery, business valuation, litigation support, expert witnessing, and cybersecurity. This chapter presents challenges and opportunities in providing fraud and nonfraud forensic accounting services. Forensic accounting is a rewarding and exciting career with much opportunities for advancements and requirements for a balanced skill sets in technical, analytical, and communication education and practice.

Action Items

1. Forensic accounting career is exciting and rewarding.
2. Opportunities in forensic accounting are abundant.
3. Forensic accounting challenges are significant.
4. Demand for and interest in fraud and nonfraud forensic accounting services are expected to continue.

Endnotes

1. *Journal of Accountancy*. 2015. "Big Data Case Study: What Forensic Accountants Need to Know." https://www.journalofaccountancy.com/issues/2015/mar/forensic-accounting-big-data-case-study.html, (accessed September 9, 2018).
2. Association of Chartered Certified Accountants (ACCA). March 1, 2017. *Demand for Forensic Accountants Is Growing*. https://www.accaglobal.com/us/en/member/member/accounting-business/2017/03/practice/forensic-accountants.html, (accessed September 24, 2018).
3. M.L. Bhasin. January, 2017. "Integrating Corporate Governance and Forensic Accounting: A Study of an Asian Country." *International Journal of Management Sciences and Business Research* 6, no. 1.
4. Deloitte. 2018. *Forensic Accountant*. https://jobs2.deloitte.com/us/en/job/DELOA003X225127/Forensic-Accountant
5. Tennessee Bureau of Investigation. 2018. *Forensic Services Division*. https://www.tn.gov/tbi/divisions/forensic-services-division.html

6. Committee of Sponsoring Organizations of the Treadway Commission (COSO). 2016. *Fraud Risk Management Guide.* https://www.coso.org/documents/COSO-Fraud-Risk-Management-Final-92816.pdf

7. Securities and Exchange Commission (SEC). May, 2013. *SEC Announces Enforcement Initiatives to Combat Financial Reporting and Microcap Fraud and Enhance Risk Analysis.* https://www.sec.gov/News/PressRelease/Detail/PressRelease/1365171624975#.UubI41NMGih

8. ACFE. 2017. *Compensation Guide for Anti-Fraud Professionals.* http://www.acfe.com/compguide-2017.aspx

9. ZipRecruiter. 2018. *Forensic Accountant Salary.* https://www.ziprecruiter.com/Salaries/Forensic-Accountant-Salary

10. Z. Rezaee, and R. Riley. 2009. *Financial Statement Fraud: Prevention and Detection* (2nd ed., Hoboken, NJ: John Wiley & Sons, Inc.)

11. COSO. 2016.

12. ACCESSDATA. 2017. *Forensic Toolkit.* https://accessdata.com/products-services/forensic-toolkit-ftk

13. Ibid.

14. C. Gomes da Silva, and P.M.R. Carreira. May, 2013. *Selecting Audit Samples Using Benford's Law. AUDITING: A Journal of Practice & Theory* 32, no. 2, pp. 53–65.

15. R.D. Cannon. 2006. "Computer Forensics for the Fraud Examiner," *ACFE.* http://www.acfe.com/article.aspx?id=4294967651

16. Board of Governors of the Federal Reserve System. 2016. *Credit and Liquidity Programs and the Balance Sheet.* http://www.federalreserve.gov/monetarypolicy/bst_riskmanagement.htm

17. Gartner. 2014. *IT Glossary.* http://www.gartner.com/it-glossary/?s=big+data, (accessed July 31, 2017).

18. L. Crumbley, L. Heitger, and S. Smith. 2015. *Forensic and Investigative Accounting* (7th ed., Chicago, IL: Commerce Clearing House).

19. Ernst and Young (EY). 2016. *Global Forensic Data Analytics Survey 2016.* http://www.ey.com/gl/en/services/assurance/fraud-investigation—dispute-services/ey-shifting-into-high-gear-mitigating-risks-and-demonstrating-returns, (accessed July 12, 2017).

20. Ibid.

21. Oracle. n.d. *What Is Data Mining?* https://docs.oracle.com/cd/ B28359_01/datamine.111/b28129/process.htm#DMCON002, (accessed September 27, 2018).

22. Oracle. n.d. *Data Warehousing Concepts.* https://docs.oracle.com/cd/ B10501_01/server.920/a96520/concept.htm, (accessed September 27, 2018).

23. Dundas. n.d. *Dundas BI Product Features.* https://www.dundas.com/ dundas-bi/features, (accessed September 27, 2018).

24. Microsoft. n.d. *What Is SharePoint?* https://support.office.com/ en-us/article/what-is-sharepoint-97b915e6-651b-43b2-827d-fb25777f446f, (accessed September 27, 2018).

25. W3. 2017. *HTML 5.2.* https://www.w3.org/TR/html52/, (Accessed September 27, 2018).

26. Public Company Accounting Oversight Board (PCAOB). "AU Section 329A—Analytical Procedures," *PCAOB.* https://pcaobus.org/ Standards/Archived/Pages/AU329A.aspx

27. S. Ransbotham, and D. Kiron. January, 2018. "Using Analytics to Improve Customer Engagement," *MIT Sloan Management Review.* http://sloanreview.mit.edu/analytics2018

28. Ibid.

29. EY. 2018. *Global Forensic Data Analytics Survey 2018.* https://assets. ey.com/content/dam/ey-sites/ey-com/global/topics/assurance/assurance-pdfs/ey-global-fda-survay.pdf, (accessed September 25, 2018).

30. Ibid.

31. BDO. 2018. *Forensic Accounting & Investigations.* https://www.bdo .com/services/business-financial-advisory/forensics-and-investigations/ overview-(1), (accessed September 25, 2018).

32. Sarbanes-Oxley Act of 2002. Section 301. http://www.sarbanes-oxley.com/section.php?level=1&pub_id=Sarbanes-Oxley

33. Ibid.

34. Sarbanes-Oxley Act, 2002. Securities and Exchange Commission (SEC). April 9, 2003. *SEC Final Rule: Standards Relating to Listed Company Audit Committees. Release Nos. 33-8220; 34-47654.* http:// www.sec.gov/rules/final/33-8220.htm

35. Ibid.

36. Ibid.

37. SOX 2002. Section 406.
38. Dodd–Frank Act of 2010.
39. Z. Rezaee. 2015. *Business Sustainability: Performance, Compliance, Accountability and Integrated Reporting* (Sheffield, UK: Greenleaf Publishing Limited).
40. NC State University. May 3, 2010. *COSO Fraud Study 2010.* https://erm.ncsu.edu/library/article/coso-fraud-study

CHAPTER 5

Emerging Issues
in Forensic Accounting

Executive Summary

Existence and persistence of high-profile financial statement fraud (FSF) can be detrimental to the integrity and soundness of the financial markets and adversely affect the quality and reliability of public financial information. Forensic accountants are well-trained and equipped to detect FSF, and thus contribute to the improvement in quality and reliability of financial reports. This chapter presents emerging issues and challenges in fraud investigation, including revenue recognition, fair value estimation, collusion and conspiracy, bribery and money laundering, and cyberattacks.

Introduction

Forensic accounting has advanced as a rewarding and exiting profession with a focus on fraud and nonfraud investigation. The area of fraud investigation has made significant progress in the past decade. However, there are still many opportunities and challenges in forensic accounting as presented in this chapter. Forensic accounting job opportunities have increased sustainability. Technological advances enable forensic accountants to use Big Data and data analytics in performing digital forensics. Challenges presented in this chapter are forensic accountants' practices in areas of proper revenue recognition, fair value estimation, bribery, money laundering, Ponzi schemes, collusion, and cybercrimes.

Fraud Investigation Challenges

This section presents many challenges associated with fraud investigation dimension of forensic accounting practices.

Forensic Accountants and Revenue Recognition

Revenue manipulation is the most common type of fraud, even though it can be very costly because of litigation, restatements, unfavorable audit reports, increased audit fees, negative market reactions, and investigations and sanctions by SEC. Any recorded revenues that do not meet the following three criteria can be alleged as fraudulent and fictitious:

1. The recorded revenues do not meet the definition of revenue as defined in Financial Accounting Standards Board (FASB) Concepts Statement 3 as "actual or expected cash inflows (or the equivalent) that have occurred or will eventually occur as a result of the enterprise's ongoing major or central operations during the period."[1]
2. They are not measurable and/or cannot be reliably measured.
3. They are not verifiable or cannot be easily verified.

In summary, firms have incentives to manipulate revenues, even though the cost of revenue manipulation may be high. Knowing the characteristics of firms that will take the chance of getting caught is important as investors, auditors, and regulators determine the riskiness attached to particular types of firms. Looking specifically at revenues and the attempts by managers to increase earnings through revenue manipulations contributes to earnings management findings by looking at the costliest form of earnings management and the characteristics of firms that are willing to suffer the high costs of this type of manipulation. These costs include litigation by shareholders, investigation and sanctions by the SEC, restatements, unfavorable audit reports with increased audit fees, and negative market reactions. In summary, empirical evidence from lawsuits, SEC enforcement actions, restatements, and audit fees show that revenue manipulations can be the costliest form of earnings management, which leads to the importance of determining the characteristics of firms that are willing to take the risks of these significant costs by manipulating revenues. The high costs associated with these firms increase the importance of these characteristics to auditors, regulators, and investors so that they can more easily determine the firms that may be tempted to increase earnings through revenue manipulations.

There are several methods of engaging in fictitious revenues. The most common method is to use fake or phantom customers in recoding fictitious revenue. The second method is to use legitimate customers and intentionally alter or inflate invoices reflecting higher amounts or quantities than actually sold. Forensic accountants can assist public companies to detect and prevent improper revenue recognition.

Fair Value Estimation

The goal of fair value accounting is to enable companies to choose whether or not to invest by showing not what the asset cost in the past, but what it would cost to buy today. The subprime scandals of 2008 can be attributed to many factors, including the improper application of fair value estimates by the real estate appraising industry. The conflicting interest between real estate appraisal firms and real estate brokerage firms provided incentives and opportunities for the appraisals to provide fair value estimates above and beyond reasonable and realistic fair value to get financing needs to close the deal. Banks had all the incentives and opportunities to get the highest fair value estimates to provide subprime loans to customers and then sell the mortgages to mortgage buyers such as Freddie Mac and Fannie Mae, quasi-government corporations established to buy up mortgages from banks. The other factor is banks' securitization vehicles of variable interest entities (VIESs) or special-purpose entities (SPEs). The appropriate tone set at the top by management regarding corporate culture within which financial reports are produced is vital to the integrity of financial reporting process. When the tone set at the top is lax, fraudulent financial reporting is more likely to occur and cannot be prevented.

The Financial Accounting Standards Board (FASB) has recently promoted the implementation of fair value principles, with no set definition for fair value. SFAS 157 defined fair value as the exchange price in an orderly transaction between market participants to sell an asset or transfer a liability in the market in which the reporting entity would transact for the asset or liability.[2] The focus is on the exit price, which is the price that would be received to sell the asset or paid to transfer the liability. SFAS 157 did not require any new fair value measurements but did provide guidance for determining the fair values of assets and liabilities and required the disclosure of information about the following: (1) the use of fair value to measure assets and the extent to which companies measure assets and liabilities at fair value; (2) the information used to measure fair value; and (3) the effect that fair value measurements have on earnings.

SFAS 157 also established a three-tiered framework for measuring fair value and dictated that the fair value of all assets and liabilities be disclosed into one of the following categories on the basis of inputs. It does, however, provide the methods for developing it. According to Financial Accounting Statement 157, information relating to the development of fair value is classified into three tiers. Level 1 inputs include prices for identical assets selling in active markets. Examples of Level 1 inputs include "US government and agency securities, foreign government debt, listed equities, and money market securities."[3] Level 2 inputs are defined as observable information on similar assets that are actively trading. Some types of Level 2 inputs are "corporate bonds (investment grade, high yield), mortgage-backed securities, bank loans, loan commitments, less liquid listed equities, municipal bonds, and certain over-the-counter derivatives."[4] Level 3 inputs are unobservable information that has been either calculated or estimated and should have the least bearing on defining the fair value of the asset. The use of the fair value method for asset valuation is an attempt by the SEC and FASB to increase the transparency and relevance of accounting information. Forensic accountants should use accounting and auditing guidelines in estimating fair values of assets and liabilities in performing valuation and economic dispute services.

Collusion and Conspiracy

Fraud often occurs because of collusion among fraudsters. Collusion can occur between executives and the board of directors and other corporate gatekeepers to mislead investors. Forensic accountants can be hired to discover collusions and conspiracy that cause fraudulent activities. Forensic

accountants should ask very detailed questions to figure out whether a
hint of wrongdoing is present. These questions are particularly addressed
to finance and accounting-related sections of the company. The reason for
this is the day-to-day responsibilities and ultimate preparation of financial data is left with these sections, and the CEO and CFO simply must
approve the statements. If forensic accountants decide that the answers
to the questions are suspicious, the team should discuss the issues with
the board and other members of the management, especially executives.[5]
Forensic accountants can use red flags to detect collusion. Common red
flags include errant payments, change in behavioral patterns, and drastic
changes in financial statement accounts. Collusion can also be conveyed
by whistle-blowing, auditing, and electronic systems.

Money Laundering

Money laundering can be defined as obtaining money from illegal activity but passing it off as having been obtained from sources of legal
and legitimate business transactions. Money laundering is the means by
which criminals, as a necessity, disguise the origin of their money so that
they may avoid the risk of prosecution. Whoever transports, transmits,
or transfers a monetary instrument or funds from a place in the United
States to or through a place outside the United States or to a place in
the United States from or through a place outside the United States as
follows:

1. with the intent to promote the carrying on of specified unlawful
   activity; or
2. knowing that the monetary instrument or funds involved in the
   transportation, transmission, or transfer represent the proceeds of
   some form of unlawful activity and knowing that such transportation, transmission, or transfer is designed in whole or in part; and
3. to conceal or disguise the nature, the location, the source, the ownership, or the control of the proceeds of specified unlawful activity.[6]

   To accomplish the above-mentioned, money laundering usually falls
into the three stages of placement, layering, and integration. Placement

occurs when unlawfully obtained money is put into financial institutions. Layering occurs when layers of complex transactions are used to separate the unlawfully obtained money from their origin. Integration occurs when legitimate transactions are used to disguise unlawfully obtained money as legitimately obtained money.[7]

To combat these stages, anti-money laundering efforts such as Suspicious Activity Reports (SARs) and Form 8300 have been put into place. SARs require financial institutions to fill out a form that brings to the IRS' attention deposits that may be irregular, or seem to intentionally avoid crossing the $10,000 threshold that would require Form 8300. Form 8300 requires that deposits of $10,000 and above be reported to the IRS. Money laundering has a corrosive effect on a country's economy, government, and social well-being. The practice distorts business decisions, increases the risk of bank failures, takes control of economic policy away from the government, harms a country's reputation, and exposes its people to drug trafficking, smuggling, and other criminal activity.[8]

The National Money Laundering Strategy was published by the U.S. Department of the Treasury, in 2000, which dictates the required government actions upon those committing money laundering.[9] These actions include identifying the seven high-risk areas, known as High-Risk Money Laundering and Financial Crimes Areas (HIFCAs), a local grant program to fund the pursuance of fraud cases in this schema.[10] A crime map is present in the financial crimes enforcement network website. The seven regional areas of high risk are California northern district, California southern district, the Southwest border, Chicago, New York, Puerto Rico, and South Florida. Each region lists specific counties or cities that have swaths of money laundering. In the Northern California district, San Francisco, Santa Cruz, and Napa are a few locations to monitor. Outside of the area map, the bill itself lists several ways to develop a framework to combat fraud. A creation of support program in high crime areas, interconnect between federal, state, and local law enforcement, and administration of grants to assist in operations are main components of the bill.[11] Forensic accountants are well-trained and have skill sets necessary to investigate money laundering.

Bribery

The Foreign Corrupt Practices Act (FCPA) of 1977 discussed in previous chapters made it illegal for U.S. companies to bribe foreign official and political parties for the purpose of advancing their business. The FCPA regulates all business conducted in the U.S. markets, regarding of country of origin. Unlike other cases of fraudulent behavior, both the public and the government feel it is necessary for companies to take direct responsibility for the occurrence of bribery. Forensic accountants can be employed to assess compliance with provisions of the FCPA in detecting and preventing corporate bribery.

In detecting bribery, risk assessment procedures, and forensic accountants can identify risk factors that may constitute the presence of bribery and fraudulent behavior. These factors include previous findings, internal control weaknesses, timing differences, geographic location, and management policies. The list of factors can be found in the source attached here.[12] After concluding that fraud may be present, substantive procedures are performed to address these risk factors. The accountant must design a strategy that can be used to change the nature and extent of further investigation. Tests are then conducted to find out specifics about detected bribery. These tests include examination of contracts, transactions, and fees; FCPA compliance; and contributions. After, the procedures have been completed, the material needs to be prepared for court. Forensic accountants use quantitative methods to measure that impact and usability of trial evidence in litigation. The forensic accounting practice is gaining in popularity due to auditor's not being able to satisfy the demand of investors and stakeholders. This has created an expectation gap that allows the growth of sophisticated fields, such as forensic accounting.[13]

Ponzi Schemes

Ponzi schemes, according to the Association of Certified Fraud Examiners (ACFE), is an illegal activity that use new investors' money to satisfy older investor's desires.[14] "Ponzi" schemes promise high financial returns or dividends not available through traditional investments. Instead of investing the funds of victims, the con artist pays "dividends" to initial investors using the funds of subsequent investors. The scheme generally falls apart when the operator flees with all the proceeds or when a sufficient number of new investors cannot be found to allow the continued payment of "dividends." This type of fraud is named after its creator Charles Ponzi of Boston, Massachusetts. In the early 1900s, Ponzi launched a scheme that guaranteed investors a 50-percent return on their investment in postal coupons. Although he was able to pay his initial backers, the scheme dissolved when he was unable to pay later investors (FBI).[15]

The best-known example of a Ponzi scheme was Bernie Madoff, a stockbroker who committed the largest Ponzi scheme in ever, estimated at a value of approximately $65 billion. Forensic accountants can assist in providing an early signal of Ponzi schemes and other fraudulent activities. Ponzi schemes are enforced by the Federal Trade Commission (FTC) and the SEC. Forensic accountants identify red flags in Ponzi schemes. The red flags include pressure tactics, little to no segregation of duties, and vows of high return and low risk. Red flags are used during investigations to alert forensic accountants to potential fraud.

Fraud and Information Technology

Organizations of different types and size invest in information technology (IT) and related resources to meet their goals and objectives. The ever-increasing use of IT and block-chain platforms and computers in data processing and the application of various enterprise systems have had significant effects on business processes and internal controls and financial reporting processes. The potential IT failure and associated business risk may cause organizations to misjudge or overlook the risk of material misstatement if they do not understand IT systems and their potentials and challenges.

Block-chain technology brings smart contracts, smarter supply chains, and the end of identity fraud. Smart contracts create "if/then" contracts between a buyer and seller. This results in one step of the selling process not being fulfilled until another step has been verified. An example of this would be purchasing an item on eBay, and having the money withdrawn from your account, but held in limbo until the item in question has been marked shipped. Then the money is released to the seller. This removes risk for the buyer in not receiving a product (service) and losing their money as well as removing risk for the seller of not getting paid after delivering a product (rendering a service).[16]

When looking at supply chains, companies can fight fraud by verifying every part of the process. For example, a diamond can be tracked from its place of origin to every hand that touches it along the way, along with serial numbers, photos, details, and documents of authenticity. As it pertains to fraud, block-chain can serve as a third-party mediator of sorts that can work in any interaction imaginable. Because a constantly reconciled ledger exists that is only updated when verified by all parties, an essential part of the fraud triangle is severely hampered—opportunity.[17] Forensic accountants should use IT platforms in performing fraud and nonfraud services.

Advancements in technology require the adoption of new skill sets by forensic accountants. Digital forensics, which includes subcategories of computer and network forensics, is an area forensic accountants work in. Digital forensics involves the use of software to analyze computer evidence. Accountants must decide what evidence is beneficial, how to protect the evidence, and how not to violate an individual's right to due process, or the Fourth Amendment of the United States Constitution. Laboratories are often used to analyze evidence and conduct substantive procedures. The evidence is used during litigation proceedings to assist to jury decisions. The rise of the Internet has led to the investigation of crimes such as intellectual property usage, child pornography, and terrorism.[18] An example of digital forensics being used to aid in capture of a criminal is the Craigslist killer, Philip Markoff. The killer hired a masseuse, Julissa Brisman, and killer her. He died in his jail cell. The police department assigned to the case tracked his IP address through Craigslist to identify him. The department also navigated his e-mail exchange between him and the masseuse. Another example of digital forensic being used to catch a criminal is Dr. Conrad Murray. He was the doctor for Michael Jackson, who died from an overdose of the drug Propofol. The forensic team investigated Dr. Murray's computer and found evidence of lethal amounts of prescriptions given to Michael Jackson. This resulted in 2 years and prison and forfeiture of his medical license.[19]

Digital forensics has seen many advances in the past 10 years. Several universities have developed curricula to teaching students the changing accounting field. West Virginia has a computer forensics program funded by Microsoft that teaches knowledge pertinent to law enforcement. The program is designed to protect against technology attacks.[20] La Salle University offers a certificate in fraud and forensic accounting. The courses required include fraud examination, occupational fraud, and cyber fraud, to name a few. Lastly, Stevenson University offers a Master's in Forensic Accounting with classes in mock trial, investigation, business valuation, and IT.

Cyberattacks and Cybercrime

A growing incident of cyber-hacking and cybersecurity breaches of information systems (e.g., Sony, Targets, JPMorgan Chase, Home Depot, and Equifax) threats sustainability of many firms and cost the U.S. economy more than $100 billion annually.[21] The Equifax cyber breach is considered as the largest data breaches in history and expected to affect nearly half of the population in the United States (about 143 million Americans).[22] Hackers were able to hack Equifax system, one of the three major consumer credit agencies, between May and July 2017 because of the weak points in its website software.[23] These initiatives and guidelines suggest that board risk oversight function, managerial strategies, and adequate IT investment and cybersecurity infrastructure could ensure the integrity of IT systems and effectiveness of cyber-infrastructure in dealing with potential cyberattacks and cybersecurity breaches. Prior research addresses several research issues of the link between IT governance, board risk oversight and managerial risk strategies, and risk management and informed risk-taking. On one hand, IT governance, board risk oversight, and managerial risk strategies can improve risk assessment and management, thus reducing cyberattacks. The International Standards Organization (ISO) 31000 defines risk as an uncertainty that has an effect on objectives. Thus, the effective board risk oversight and managerial risk strategies are expected to improve cyberattacks risk management, reducing cyber-hacking incidents that benefit the firm and its stakeholders.

Managerial risk strategies and practices can effectively reduce the incidents of cyberattacks. However, recent centralization of operations

and information system Internet-based technologies to improve cost efficiency and effectiveness across supply chain creates security risks and
high exposure to and dependency on the Internet that provide opportunities for cyber hackers to engage in rewarding cyberattacks. Centralization
across organization functions requires the use of sophisticated operations
technology (OT) and IT with related network infrastructure to connect
geographically diverse functions. Thus, managerial risk strategies pertaining to both OT and IT securities and controls are become increasingly
important under centralized system to prevent hackers to penetrate the
system and engage in costly cyberattacks. However, many OT and IT
security programs are old, underdeveloped, and outdated that give incentives and opportunities to cyber attacker to perpetrate these programs and
engage in costly cyber-hacking activities. Managerial risk strategies and
programs are initially designed to identify the emerging cyber-hackings or
information security threats and implement risk assessment and internal
control procedures to immediately respond to such hackings and security
breaches. Any outdated and underdeveloped OT and IT can provide incentives and opportunities to cyber attackers to perpetrate business systems and programs and cause costly cyber-hacking activities.

Given the importance of the cybersecurity and IT risks, it is likely
that corporate board either already has a director who is well-versed in IT
and data security or is looking for one to help better understand the company's IT risk profile. The Information Security Booklet of the Federal
Financial Institutions Examination Council (FFIEC) suggests several cybersecurity oversight and management activities including the following:
(1) existence of a risk compliance board committee or executive position
such as chief information officer (CIO); (2) implementation and management of the information security and business continuity programs
by the designated executive or board committee; (3) annual report to the
board of directors or designated board committee by management on the
overall status of the business continuity programs and information security; and (4) the existence of budgeting process for information security
investments and related expenses and annual review and approval by the
board of directors.[24]

Implemented OT and IT security programs are designed to identify
security threats and cyberattacking information and assess their risk and

related internal controls to effectively respond to any security breaches and hackings. Any risk associated with cyberattacks should be effectively and timely assessed, and proper information security strategies should be designed and implemented to combat cyberattacks. Establishing tone at the top of effective oversight by the board of directors and management strategies is vital in combatting cyberattacks. The board can oversee managerial risk strategies and practices and obtain an understanding of risks inherent in managerial strategies for risk appetite and access timely information on risk appetite, risk response strategies, and effective risk assessment and management. Forensic accountants can assist the board of directors and management in their proper risk assessment and management.

Fraud risk assessment is the process of using a framework to identify risks that can lead to fraud. Organizations such as COSO have released models that aid in assessing and managing fraud risk. Fraud risk assessment contains three main elements: inherent risk, assess inherent risk, and response to inherent and residual risk. Identifying inherent risk surveys the fraud triangle (incentives, pressures, opportunities) specific to the organization and its connection to fraud schemes and internal control. Second, assess the chance of fraud occurring from observation of data and business processes. Interviews of staff and management occur during this phase. Lastly, an appropriate response to the assessed risk should be chosen after analysis is done. The analysis weighs cost and benefit of implementing corrective controls to the apparent risks. All the above-mentioned elements should appear within a fraud risk assessment framework. This framework is designed by the organization and can include categories such as identified risks, effectiveness of controls, response, and impact. The risk assessment is often done across departments to fill out an entire portfolio view of the business and maintain full integration with business processes.[25]

Fraud risk assessment processes include the following steps:

Step 1. Identify your business processes
The possibility for fraud starts with business processes. In order to properly assess fraud risk, processes must be identified.

Step 2. Consider differences in those processes in foreign operations, as well as among subsidiaries or decentralized divisions

Step 3. Identify the "Process Owner" for each of the identified processes

Step 4. Review fraud experience within the company and by process

Step 5. Process Owners identify how fraud may occur in each process at each location using Fraud Brainstorming Techniques

Step 6. Identify the Parties who have the ability to commit the potential fraud

Step 7. Process Owners evaluate the likelihood that each of the identified frauds could occur

Step 8. Determine the level of mitigation so as to prevent, detect, and deter fraud

Step 9. Investigate the characteristics of potential fraud manifestations within each process identified

Step 10. Quantify Fraud Risk

Despite being clearly outlined, fraud risk assessment has its pitfalls. Approximately 25 percent of companies still use the 1992 framework or have not revealed which framework they have followed. As a result, the SEC has issued the statement saying, "The longer [corporate] issuers continue to use the 1992 framework, the more likely they are to receive questions from the [SEC] staff about whether the issuer's use of the 1992 framework satisfies the SEC's requirement to use a suitable, recognized framework."[26] Some organizations underestimate the time and effort required to properly plan for a fraud risk assessmen (FRA)t. Companies should be weary of not planning ahead to allow for an adequate amount of time and should ensure that relevant stakeholders are involved in the FRA process. Companies often invest a significant amount of time identifying controls for relevant fraud schemes, without noticing that those schemes are of minor impact to the organization even if they occur repeatedly. Companies should note that FRA is not a one-shot item. The landscape is constantly evolving and they must reassess to keep up. Insufficient documentation may make it difficult for a company to show to regulators or auditors that they have adequately met the requirements of the 2013 COSO framework.[27]

Ever-increasing incidents of cyberattacks are devastating to business organizations' operations, governance, financial reporting, and audit processes.

Cyberattacks at companies such as Sony, Targets, Yahoo, JPMorgan Chase, Uber, Home Depot, Equifax, Facebook threaten their business sustainability. Regulatory initiatives and guidelines are being developed in assisting public companies and their directors and officers to understand, identify, assess, and manage risks of corporate cybersecurity. For example, the Securities and Exchange Commission (SEC) established several initiatives of guidelines on cybersecurity disclosures, enforcement actions against several public companies for cyber-related hacking, and an investigatory report concerning internal control failures relevant to cyberattacks.[28] The growing cyberattacks create opportunities for forensic accountants to assist business organizations in assessing their cybersecurity risks and design proper internal controls to prevent, detect, and correct cyberattacks. Forensic accountants can also engage in damage controls and appropriate disclosure of cyberattacks.

Conclusion

Forensic accounting has made significant progress in the past decades and will continue to add value in many aspects of business, particularly in the areas of fraud and nonfraud investigation. This chapter presents challenges and opportunities in providing fraud investigation. Forensic accounting is a rewarding and exciting career with many opportunities for advancements as discussed in this chapter. Forensic accountants should turn challenges into job opportunities in providing fraud and nonfraud investigation services.

Action Items

1. Forensic accounting career is rewarding and exiting with superb job opportunities.
2. Forensic accounting challenges are significant in the areas of fraud investigation.
3. Demand for and interest in fraud and nonfraud forensic accounting investigation services are expected to continue.
4. Forensic accountants should turn the challenges into job opportunities in fraud investigation services.

Endnotes

1. Financial Accounting Standards Board (FASB). 1980. *Status of Concepts Statements No.3.* https://www.fasb.org/status/statpg-con3.shtml

2. Financial Accounting Standards Board (FASB). 2006. *Statement of Financial Accounting Standards No. 157: Fair Value Measurements* (September, 2006). https://www.fasb.org/summary/stsum157.shtml

3. Statement of Financial Accounting Standards No. 157. Financial Accounting Standards Board. 2006.

4. Ibid.

5. G.D. Moore, and S.R. Mark. April, 2016. "Fraud, Collusion and the Financial Statements-A Refresher for Practicing Professionals," *Journal of Global Business Management* 12, no. 1. http://www.jgbm.org/page/16%20Gail%20D%20Moore.pdf

6. Federal Deposit Insurance Corporation (FDIC). 2009. *Bank Secrecy Act and Anti-Money Laundering.* https://www.fdic.gov/regulations/examinations/bsa/index.html

7. J. McDowell, and G. Novis. 2001. *The Consequences of Money Laundering and Financial Crime.* https://www.hsdl.org/?view&did=3549, (accessed July 18, 2018).

8. Ibid.

9. US Department of the Treasury. January 1, 2001. *Guidance on Enhanced Scrutiny for Transactions That May Involve the Proceeds of Foreign Official Corruption.* https://www.treasury.gov/press-center/press-releases/Pages/guidance.aspx

10. HSDL. March 2, 2000. *The National Money Laundering Strategy for 2000.* https://www.hsdl.org/?view&did=439771

11. Congress. 1998. *H.R. 1756—Money Laundering and Financial Crimes Strategy Act of 1998.* https://www.congress.gov/bill/105th-congress/house-bill/1756

12. Ibid.

13. Ibid.

14. ACFE. n.d. *Ponzi Schemes.* http://www.acfe.com/ponzi-schemes.aspx

15. FBI. n.d. *Scams and Safety.* http://www.fbi.gov/scams-safety/fraud

16. Forbes. 2018. *3 Ways Blockchain Can Help Combat Fraud.* https://www.forbes.com/sites/danielnewman/2018/04/17/3-ways-blockchain-can-help-combat-fraud/#4f46c76a92a4

17. Ibid.

18. M.A. Crain, W.S. Hopwood, C. Pacini, and G.R. Young. 2015. *Essentials of Forensic Accounting* (New York, NY: AICPA).

19. Rasmussen College. 2018. *Cracking Cases with Digital Forensics.* https://www.rasmussen.edu/degrees/justice-studies/blog/cracking-cases-with-digital-forensics/, (accessed September 18, 2018).

20. West Virginia. 2018. *Computer Forensics.* https://graduateadmissions.wvu.edu/academics/graduate-programs/computer-forensics-gc

21. Center for Strategic and International Studies (CSIS). July 7, 2013. *The Economic Impact of Cyber Crime and Cyber Espionage.* Available at https://www.csis.org/analysis/economic-impact-cybercrime

22. L.J. SternbergJ. September 14, 2017. "Surviving the Equifax Data Breach," *AICPA Insights.* http://blog.aicpa.org/2017/09/surviving-the-equifax-data-breach.html?cm_em=zrezaee@memphis.edu&cm_mmc=AICPA:CheetahMail-_-NewsUpdate-_-SEP17-_-AICPA NewsUpdate_A17SP136_IMTA#sthash.JuRiR7ZH.dpbs

23. Ibid.

24. Federal Financial Institutions Examination Council (FFIEC). June, 2015. *IT Examination Hand Book InfoBase.* http://ithandbook.ffiec.gov/it-booklets/information-security.aspx; https://www.ffiec.gov/cyberassessmenttool.htm

25. AICPA. n.d. *Managing the Business Risk of Fraud: A Practical Guide.* https://www.aicpa.org/forthepublic/auditcommitteeeffectiveness/auditcommitteebrief/downloadabledocuments/managing_the_business_risk_of_fraud.pdf, (accessed September 18, 2018).

26. Deloitte. 2015. *Fraud Risk Assessments and COSO's 2013 Internal Control Framework: Opportunities and Common Pitfalls.* https://www2.deloitte.com/content/dam/Deloitte/us/Documents/finance/us-fas-fra-coso-article.pdf, (accessed July 19, 2018).

27. Ibid.

28. Securities and Exchange Commission (SEC). (2018). *Commission Statement and Guidance on Public Company Cybersecurity Disclosures.* Release Nos. 33-1059; 34-82746, February 26, 2018. https://www.sec.gov/rules/interp/2018/33-10459.pdf

About the Author

Dr. Zabihollah (Zabi) Rezaee, PhD, CPA, CMA, CIA, CFE, CGFM, CSOXP, CGOVP, CGRCP, CGMA, and CRMA is the Thompson-Hill Chair of Excellence, PhD coordinator and professor of accountancy at the University of Memphis and has served a two-year term on the Standing Advisory Group (SAG) of the Public Company Accounting Oversight Board (PCAOB). He received his BS degree from the Iranian Institute of Advanced Accounting, his MBA from Tarleton State University in Texas, and his PhD from the University of Mississippi. He holds 10 certifications, including Certified Public Accountant (CPA), Certified Fraud Examiner (CFE), Certified Management Accountant (CMA), Certified Internal Auditor (CIA), Certified Government Financial Manager (CGFM), Certified Sarbanes-Oxley Professional (CSOXP), Certified Corporate Governance Professional (CGOVP), Certified Governance Risk Compliance Professional (CGRCP), Chartered Global Management Accountant (CGMA), and Certified Risk Management Assurance (CRMA). He served as the 2012–2014 secretary of the Forensic Accounting (FIA) Section of the American Accounting Association (AAA) and is currently serving on Auditing Standards Committee of the Auditing Section of the AAA. He was one of the finalists for the position of the Faculty Trustee at the University of Memphis in 2016 and the Ombudsperson position in 2017. He is the incoming editor of the *Journal of Forensic Accounting Research* of the AAA (2019–2020). He has served as expert witness and testified in federal courts.

Rezaee has published over 220 articles, made more than 230 presentations, and has written 11 book chapters. He has also published 12 books: *Financial Institutions, Valuations, Mergers, and Acquisitions: The Fair Value Approach*; *Financial Statement Fraud: Prevention and Detection*; *U.S. Master Auditing Guide* 3rd edition; *Audit Committee Oversight Effectiveness*

Post-Sarbanes–Oxley Act; *Corporate Governance Post-Sarbanes–Oxley: Regulations, Requirements, and Integrated Processes*; *Corporate Governance and Business Ethics and Financial Services Firms: Governance, regulations, Valuations, Mergers and Acquisitions,* and contributed to several other books. His two recent books on *Corporate Sustainability: Integrating Performance and Reporting,* published in November 2012, won the 2013 Axiom Gold Award in the category of Business Ethics and *Business Sustainability: Performance, Compliance, Accountability, and Integrated Reporting* was published in October 2015 by Greenleaf Publishing. The book on *Audit Committee Effectiveness* was published in three volumes by Business Expert Press in July 2016. His most recent books are on *Corporate Governance in the Aftermath of the Global Financial Crisis*, in four volumes, published by Business Expert Press in March 2018 and *Business Sustainability in Asia,* published by John Wiley and Sons in March 2019. Several of these books are translated into other languages including Chinese, Persian, Korean, and Spanish.

Index

OTHER TITLES IN OUR FINANCIAL ACCOUNTING, AUDITING AND TAXATION COLLECTION

Mark S. Bettner, Bucknell University; Michael P. Coyne, Fairfield University; and Roby Sawyers, *Editors*

- *Accounting History and the Rise of Civilization, Volume I* by Gary Giroux
- *Accounting History and the Rise of Civilization, Volume II* by Gary Giroux
- *A Refresher in Financial Accounting* by Faisal Sheikh
- *Accounting Fraud, Second Edition: Maneuvering and Manipulation, Past and Present* by Gary Giroux
- *Corporate Governance in the Aftermath of the Global Financial Crisis, Volume I: Relevance and Reforms* by Zabihollah Rezaee
- *Corporate Governance in the Aftermath of the Global Financial Crisis, Volume II: Functions and Sustainability* by Zabihollah Rezaee
- *Corporate Governance in the Aftermath of the Global Financial Crisis, Volume III: Gatekeeper Functions* by Zabihollah Rezaee
- *Corporate Governance in the Aftermath of the Global Financial Crisis, Volume IV: Emerging Issues in Corporate Governance* by Zabihollah Rezaee
- *Using Accounting & Financial Information, Second Edition: Analyzing, Forecasting, and Decision Making* by Mark S. Bettner
- *Pick a Number, Second Edition: The U.S. and International Accounting* by Roger Hussey
- *The Story Underlying the Numbers: A Simple Approach to Comprehensive Financial Statements Analysis* by S. Veena Iyer
- *Forensic Accounting and Financial Statement Fraud, Volume I: Fundamentals of Forensic Accounting* by Zabihollah Rezaee

Announcing the Business Expert Press Digital Library

Concise e-books business students need for classroom and research

This book can also be purchased in an e-book collection by your library as

- *a one-time purchase,*
- *that is owned forever,*
- *allows for simultaneous readers,*
- *has no restrictions on printing, and*
- *can be downloaded as PDFs from within the library community.*

Our digital library collections are a great solution to beat the rising cost of textbooks. E-books can be loaded into their course management systems or onto students' e-book readers. The **Business Expert Press** digital libraries are very affordable, with no obligation to buy in future years. For more information, please visit **www.businessexpertpress.com/librarians**. To set up a trial in the United States, please email **sales@businessexpertpress.com**.

www.ingramcontent.com/pod-product-compliance
Lightning Source LLC
Chambersburg PA
CBHW061313220326
41599CB00026B/4856